One Single Reason

Conversations with Single Women

MICHELLE J. GOFF

Minnie
God's blessings
and peace upon
you in your single
journey
again
Love & hugs —
M J Goff

Iron Rose Sister Ministries
Searcy, Arkansas

Michelle J. Goff / Kindle Direct Publishing
Iron Rose Sister Ministries
www.IronRoseSister.com
1-501-593-4849

Book Layout ©2013 BookDesignTemplates.com

One Single Reason / Michelle J. Goff.—1st ed.
ISBN 978-1-7340293-6-9

*Dedicated to all the single ladies
who have faithfully contributed
to this conversation and patiently
awaited this book. You are my heroes.*

Preface

This book cannot begin to capture the breadth and depth of the topic of singleness, nor was that my original intent. Whether discussed in our church buildings, across our kitchen tables, or in coffee shops, the primary goal has been to facilitate a broader and deeper conversation on this topic.

And the one single reason for doing so? Love.

Out of deep love for my single sisters and their constant requests that I author a book like this...

Out of the same deep love for my married friends who long to know how to better support their single sisters...

Out of pained love for the countless young women who are hurting from the world's bombardment of lies and damaging messages...

Out of profound love for other faithful, Christian single women who are weary...

Out of redeeming love for single women who are unsure about their way back to church, or even to God...

And out of the unparalleled love demonstrated by our loving heavenly Father through sending His Son and honoring us with the indwelling of His Spirit...

I humbly offer you a glimpse into these imperfect and perpetually incomplete conversations with single women. Thanks for joining in the journey.

Michelle J. Goff

09-06-2022

Contents

Introduction

09-06-2022

Sarah Andrews knew her mission. Sarah Andrews felt her calling. At the age of 23, she left home on Christmas Day, boarding a boat as a single woman missionary headed to Japan in 1915. Over the next 45 years, even during World War II, Sarah stayed and served in Japan, only returning to the U.S. for brief respites to regain her health. Her work began in partnership with other missionaries in the area, but she remained when others left, deepening her dedication and relationships with the Japanese people.

She remained in Japan throughout World War II, first in a prison camp, from which she was released in September 1942 because of a lack of provisions, then under house arrest for the remainder of the war. Of her war experience, she later wrote, "I had never experienced hunger until I was caught in the throes of war and famine as an enemy national during this war."[1]

During her time in Japan, she was instrumental in establishing four churches in Japan and witnessed them grow into four more, totaling eight congregations. The Japanese people's respect for Sarah grew through her commitment to the Japanese and her tenacity to remain in country through the war. Her personal sacrifice is exemplary, and her humble words illustrate the motivation behind her dedication.

---

[1] Hughes, Richard T. and R. L. Roberts. "Andrews, Sarah Shepherd (26 November 1893, Dickson, TN—16 September, 1961, Japan). Education: Dickson College. Career: Missionary." *The Churches of Christ.* (Wesport, CT: Greenwood Publishing Group. 2001), 165-66.

After the war a friend asked her, "Why did you stay?" Andrews responded, "If I had not been in Japan... the three churches in my section of the country, together with the property, would have been lost to the national federation of churches. Therefore, I rejoice to have stayed and suffered for the cause of truth."[2]

To say that Christ's love compelled this single woman missionary would be an understatement. Even after her post-war convalescence in the U.S., Sarah was determined to return to Japan. "To give Japan the gospel is the answer to its greatest need and service to others."[3] At the root of Sarah's motivation was her love for God and her love for the Japanese people. **Love was her one single reason.**

Verses like John 3:16 summarize the sacrificial love demonstrated throughout the pages of the Bible. God's eternal love story is an invitation for us to return His love and share it with others. In the same way that He lived out love, ultimately through the sacrifice of His Son, we are challenged to live out love as our singular motivation, even to the point of sacrificing our personal desires.

When Jesus faced the cross, torn by His conflicting desires, He was motivated by the same single reason of love. As the apostle John says in his gospel, Jesus affirms and clarifies that reason—His love for His Father and for the people He was to save. *"Now my soul is troubled, and what shall I say? 'Father, save me from this hour'? No, it was for this very reason I came to this hour. Father, glorify your name!"* (John 12:27-28a, NIV)

Expressions of "for this reason," "for this purpose," or "for this cause" in Scripture offer insight into the "why" behind a decision or next course of action. In many instances, "for this reason" can be

---

[2] Hughes, Richard T. and R. L. Roberts. "Andrews, Sarah Shepherd (26 November 1893, Dickson, TN—16 September, 1961, Japan). Education: Dickson College. Career: Missionary." *The Churches of Christ.* (Wesport, CT: Greenwood Publishing Group. 2001), 165-66.

[3] Sarah Andrews, "Reports and Plans of Work in Japan," *Gospel Advocate* November 1947, 950.

translated "therefore" or "because of this..." as an invitation to look back to the cause or reason alluded to by the author or the speaker.

"For this reason he had to be made like them, fully human in every way..."
(Heb. 2:17, NIV)

"For this reason, since the day we heard about you, we have not stopped praying for you." (Col. 1:9, NIV)

In other instances, the phrase "for this reason..." details an explanation or motivation within the word itself, as in Ephesians 3. The phrase is translated from the Greek word, *charin*, whose root is *charis*, meaning, "grace as a gift or blessing." *"For this reason I, Paul, the prisoner of Christ Jesus for the sake of you Gentiles... For this reason I kneel before the Father,"* (Eph. 3:1, 14, NIV). Out of grace-filled lovingkindness, Paul invited the Ephesians to know the same love of God he had come to know, and then live out that love among each other in the church.

An outpouring of God's love and a motivation of love for others are at the root of each of the aforementioned reasons ("therefore" or *charin*). **For this reason (therefore) and for this reason (grace, lovingkindness, and favor through Christ), God has given us our one single reason to engage in conversation with single women: Our love for God and love for others.** We live out love for God and for others when we are first filled to overflowing by His love.

It is my prayer that we never lose sight of God's nor our one single reason: love.

It was for this one single reason that Sarah Andrews became a pioneering single woman missionary and lived out love as a Christian in Japan.

It was for this one single reason that single women, on the pages of this book, will share their own stories of struggle, victory, frustration, and redemption.[4]

It is for this one single reason that others, who are not single women, have picked up this book—to love, listen, and learn.

Love is the best "one single reason" for everything. **And love is best defined in relationship with God and relationship with one another— not exclusively in the context of marriage.** Yet the perceived pressure the church puts on women to marry and have children can leave a single woman feeling unaccepted and unsupported.

If it all comes back to love, ladies, let's learn how to love God, love others, and love ourselves as single women.

We will begin our discussion with those who are **Single and Lovin' It, Mostly**, laying the groundwork statistically, biblically, and practically (Section I). The following four sections will address **Supporting One Another** (II), **Identifying the Deepest Desires of Our Heart** (III), **Avoiding the CAJE Traps** (IV), and how to reach contentment by **Responding APTLY** (V).

Some sections or stories may not feel as relatable to you personally. The Table Talk chapter at the end of each section will offer the opportunity to hear others' stories and perspectives—not to mention the opportunity to share your own.

We will conclude our conversation with specific **Congregational Strategies** (Section VI). Then finally, for those who are interested, Section VII, **Next Level Discussions**, will guide you through how to make this book a small group discussion, as well as share the initial and follow-up survey and interview questions. A summary of other research methods and findings are available upon request.

---

[4] Some women's names have been changed, per their request.

Thank you for joining in the conversation! Pull up a chair and let's get started.

Section I

Single and Lovin' It, Mostly

> [7] *I wish that all were as I myself am. But each has his own gift from God,*
> *one of one kind and one of another.* [8] *To the unmarried and the widows*
> *I say that it is good for them to remain single, as I am.* (1 Cor. 7:7-8, ESV) *Really why?*

I love to watch people's facial expressions when I proudly state, "I'm single and lovin' it!" The statement is initially met with mixed reviews then, after a brief pause, I say the final word, "mostly." An inquisitive tilt of the head follows their chuckle, but before they can verbalize their question, I quickly respond, "I am just trying to be honest." I continue with a disclaimer appropriate to the audience: older or younger, married or single, men or women. **Somewhere inside my head, I feel the need to justify the fact that I am still single.**

The same spirit of disclaimer, constant caveats, and gentle apologies riddle the pages of most books written by singles on this topic, especially when written by single women. I have often found myself wishing the author would just say what she needs to say without adding the conditional statements acknowledging the other side of the argument, but then I realize that I do the same thing.

The defensive or overly explanatory position from which many single and single-again women must express themselves indicates one problem that I pray this book will address: a perceived lack of understanding or heartfelt love for single and single-again women, especially inside the church.

It is easy to get caught up in the secondary justifications and lengthy explanations when we are challenged to live out love toward others, especially when addressing the topic of singleness from a biblical perspective or in a church context.

• Yes, marriage is awesome and God-ordained. But so is being single! What about Paul, Miriam, Nehemiah, Mary, Martha, and many other biblical examples of God's single servants?

• Yes, purity is a priority and God wants to protect us from the repercussions of impurity. Yet, He is also a God of redemption and

7

forgiveness. Didn't Jesus say, "May He who is without sin cast the first stone"?

• Yes, the family is the lifeblood and the center of our churches. But family is not always defined as a husband, wife, and 2.5 kids. What of the single sister who feels called to foster, then adopt special needs children, for example?

• Yes, God hates divorce and the destruction it causes. But even God recognizes that it cannot always be avoided. How can we minister to children and single moms whose worlds have been turned upside down by the ravages of a divorce they never wanted in the first place?

Do you have a story that feels less lovable or that you feel a constant need to defend?

No matter the dynamics of his/her story, every single person, and not just the singles, wants to be heard, valued, understood, included, invited, and given the opportunity to serve. However, for anyone who feels marginalized, especially in our churches, this comes with a myriad of uphill battles and untold challenges.

Through the pages of this book, I hope to facilitate a conversation that takes us back to the one single reason that truly motivates us all: love—love for God and love for others. And if you struggle with loving yourself as a single or single-again woman, I am especially speaking to you.

So, pull up a chair while I chat with my single girlfriends—yes, I'm talking to you! Everyone is invited to have a seat at the table. I pray that through the stories shared and the scriptural insights offered on this topic, **we will each come to know and be known by having a voice in the conversation.**

These are not easy conversations. Rather, they are often awkward. Yet no one has died from awkwardness. Actually, most people I know, after they have gotten past the awkwardness, have come to a beautiful depth of relationship together, through sincere love, transparent communication, and vulnerable openness, that can only be experienced on the other side of that tension.

So, please have the chuckle-filled response to the title of this first section. I hope it relieves some of the tension that this topic automatically generates, but let's not stop there. Let's lean into that tension. This often-untouched subject is even more rarely celebrated; therefore, I invite you to listen, love, and learn as we rejoice in what God can teach us through these conversations.

Remember that love, for God and others, is our one single reason to listen and engage in the awkward.

CHAPTER 1

With out a husband =

How do you define singles?

"You keep using that word. I do not think it means what you think it means."
(Iñigo, The Princess Bride)[5] *Really*

In its simplest form for church contexts, a single person is someone who is not currently married. However, was this individual married at some point previously? Does she have children? Is she widowed? Does the young professional college

---

[5] *The Princess Bride*, directed by Rob Reiner. (Twentieth Century Fox Film Corporation, 1987).

09-07-2022

graduate have the same "single" status as the divorced woman without kids? And what of those who choose to be single versus those who long to find a spouse? Contented singles or frustrated ones?

Singles. In a society that celebrates individuality, we cannot possibly highlight all of the variations and nuances to each person's specific story. As we make generalized comments that traffic in stereotypes, the greatest encouragement is to build relationships with members of the body from diverse walks of life.

Furthermore, my greatest admonition is that we seek God's voice in this conversation. Let's make sure His seat is at the head of the table. When I focus on the points that society and even church culture make on this topic, I get discouraged and frustrated. When I listen to the many single women who feel their voices have never been heard, I am burdened by their pain. Yet, this is a burden that is worth sharing. *"Bear one another's burdens, and so fulfill the law of Christ"* (Gal. 6:2, ESV).

Even when there were parts of the conversation that were difficult, the single women I've interviewed appreciated the opportunity to share their stories. **Giving someone a voice in the conversation is a way of sharing the burden of her difficulty and lightening her load.** And remember, it is a burden we were not designed to carry alone.

[28] "Come to me, all you who are weary and burdened, and I will give you rest. [29] Take my yoke upon you and learn from me, for I am gentle and humble in heart, and you will find rest for your souls. [30] For my yoke is easy and my burden is light." (Matt. 11:28-30, NIV)

Until I step back into God's Word and allow His lens to give me a clearer perspective, the weight of others' words is unbearable and overwhelming. The truths in Scripture will be our guide as we tackle this topic. His Word does not change (Heb. 13:5; James 1:17). It is a constant through the shifts in society—and there have been significant shifts in the culture for single women.

For the purposes of the surveys, interviews, and associated conversations for the research of this book, **the terms "single" and** "single-again" have been adopted to mean "never married" (single) or "divorced, separated, or widowed" (single-again). A separate question was asked regarding whether the woman was a parent or guardian. One hundred and sixty-five (165) single or single-again English-speaking women were surveyed from 26 states across the U.S., and six who live in other countries as missionaries. Fifty-five (55) Spanish-speaking singles were surveyed from across the Americas. For a complete copy of the survey questions and additional stats (220 total women surveyed), see Section VII, Next Level Discussions.

This book will primarily use the singular term "single," but will be intentional about highlighting the myriad of applications of that term. There are no blanket statements that apply to everyone, unless we are talking about members of the body and participants in the Kingdom... hmm... maybe we will come to recognize more of what every single one of us has in common.

Using a play on words, what are some of the things that every single person (everyone) has in common, regardless of marital status?

what do you mean?

Go ahead and re-read the question. I'll wait while you answer it.

In honor of the conversational style I have adopted for each of the Bible study books I have written, I will frequently share a question or two for personal reflection, then pick back up my part of the conversation. You can picture me pausing to take a sip of water as I ask for some feedback and input from you before continuing.

I encourage you to make notes and refer to some of your own reflections as you interact with the material and later engage even more people in the conversation. To that same end, at the conclusion of all seven sections (after Chapter 4 for Section I), there will be a segment entitled Table Talk. Each section's wrap up will include Talk with God (Reflection Questions), Talk with an Iron Rose Sister (the Common Threads), Table Talk with One Another (for one-on-one or small group discussion) and Walk the Talk. As with this next question, you also can use these questions inserted within the chapters as invitations for others to share their input.

Out of love for God and their Christian sisters in all walks of life, a diverse group of women have participated in pilot group discussions and reviews of this book—married and single, young and old, black, white, and Hispanic. **One of the most beautiful outcomes has been the love expressed even through misunderstandings and the lack of awareness on all sides.** Truly, love does cover over a multitude of sins (1 John 4:18). Let's live out love and keep our one single reason going as we open the conversation up to a broader group of women. Thank you for joining in this dialogue. You are welcome here.

What is your one single reason for picking up this book, and what do you most hope to glean from the book and subsequent conversations?

Are you ready? I have saved you a seat at the table.

Read: ended 09-07-2022

CHAPTER 2

09-07-2022

A Seat at the Table

T he anticipation of a five-day conference with a group of Christian women at a nice hotel was palpable. Before the fifty participants arrived, the twenty team members gathered for a couple of days of prayer and preparation. Even after having met only one time previously, women were chatting and reminiscing like long-lost relatives at a family reunion.

Knowing all of my food allergies and intolerances, the team had helped make prior arrangements for me to stay in one of the hotel rooms with a small kitchen. Grateful for the accommodation, I was determined to make the best of my room on the other side of the hotel's campus from where the rest of the group was staying. We agreed that I would prepare my foods ahead of time, then carry my meal to eat at the table with the entire group, especially to enjoy the time of fellowship.

Before the first meal, I confirmed the plan regarding mealtime with the organizers. Still, when I arrived in the dining room and counted the chairs around the elegantly decorated table, I quickly realized that I did not have a seat.

Awkwardly balancing my reheated meal in my hands, I dragged a chair from a nearby table and sat as inconspicuously as possible on the corner. The hotel staff was less-than-pleased with what I had done. I worked to explain what had been previously arranged, all while attempting to welcome the other women who were arriving. Of course, they chose to start filling the seats at the opposite end of the table.

My inner middle-school child cowered, feeling sorely out of place. Deepest fears of being left out, not picked, not measuring up, or not having a place flooded my mind. No matter how much I recognized the spiritual attack and worked not to give Satan the last word, my feelings of inadequacy and exclusion bubbled to the surface along with my tears.

Assured that the issue had been remedied and that I would have a seat at the table from that point forward, I swallowed a big glass of water, attempting to swallow my tears and squelch my feelings. I was not going to let this disappointment dominate my afternoon, nor this one episode taint the anticipation of the overall event.

Except, the same thing happened three more times. Yes, for the following three meals, I had no seat at the table. Determined not to let it get the best of me, for the final meal, I pulled up a chair to the corner of the table and moved a place setting from a middle seat at the long table down to that corner spot. Seating myself in the middle of the table, I put on my best mask of self-confidence and prayed that the person at the corner seat did not feel as awkward as I had felt for the previous three meals. At least she had a place setting.

Are you feeling the injustice of my plight and the awkwardness of the situation? It truly felt like a spiritual battle being waged at every meal. In a similar sense, **the feeling of not having a seat at the table is how many single and single-again women feel every time they walk into a church building or church gathering.**

We are not here to point fingers or place blame. However, it is important to recognize the perceived reality of what church is for many of the single individuals in our lives.

Around half of the population in the United States is single or single-again.[6] Is that the same makeup of our congregations? Why or why not?

From an evangelistic perspective, if we were to invite more than half of the population to visit our church, would they feel like they have a place at the Lord's table? *Its according to how they present themselves*

The table we gather at on Sunday mornings and the table around which we are having this conversation is not "singles only." If you are married and reading this, we invite you to pull up a chair and have a chat with me and my single friends. Thank you for allowing us to have a voice in this conversation and facilitate how we can productively and genuinely move forward toward the love that God longs for us to reflect in each other's lives. And I invite you to continue this authentic conversation without me by developing relationships with single and single-again women in your area, not as a project, but as a sincere opportunity to listen and learn. As the body of Christ, we each have something to give, and we need every member of the body, with Christ as the head, to make us whole. *Amen = we need give Christ what is due Him, He comes first in our lives and everything else falls into place*

---

[6] Bureau of Labor and Statistics Study in 2014 reported that 50.2% of the 124.6 million American adults were single, compared to 22% in 1976. Depending on the study cited and age range considered, anywhere from 31-51% of the U.S. population is currently unmarried. Other contributing factors are race, education, and sexual orientation (Anna Brown, "A profile of single Americans" (Pew Research, Social Trends 2020: https://www.pewsocialtrends.org/2020/08/20/a-profile-of-single-americans).

09-07-2022

Who Is Facilitating This Conversation? O'Jree

I am a single woman, never married. It is a part of who I am, and it shapes a significant part of how I view life, do life, and interact with others. I truly am "Single and Lovin' It, Mostly."

Singleness is one of the lenses through which I filter my perceptions; therefore, I would be remiss in neglecting to acknowledge the inherent bias that comes with that facet of who I am.

One of the motivations behind this book is to illuminate the fact that, especially in church culture, we may not recognize the biases or lenses through which we communicate and relate with others. For example, any time I am afforded the opportunity to speak publicly, my single sisters are the first to amen because they feel represented in illustrations and lesson topics; also true for Bible study materials I write.

However, being a single woman is not what defines who I am. A unicorn of sorts, I am a single Christian woman who has had the blessing, honor, and challenge of devoting her entire career to serving in full-time ministry in various contexts within the churches of Christ, across the world.

If I were to pick three words to describe myself, my first three words would be "Ah! Only three?" followed quickly by a request to give me more than just three words! From an early age, I have been expressive and verbal. I have been told more than once that I have "the gift of gab." The oldest of four girls, my pioneering spirit has served to break the ice and blaze a trail that others might follow. Loud, verbose, energetic, joyful, a champion of the marginalized, a Spanish nerd, an Atlanta Braves and LSU Tigers fan, a Latina at heart... no matter how you describe me, my prayer is that my love for God, for others, and for myself will be my lasting legacy. It truly is my one single reason.

Growing up in the church, my faith background and religious cultural context shaped many of my initial observations and perceptions, especially since my dad was the deacon for the singles' ministry for nine years when my sisters and I were young, in Baton Rouge, Louisiana. I later returned to that same town to work in Campus Ministry, attain my master's degree, and continue my fandom for the LSU Tigers.

My undergraduate degree was obtained at Harding University, a private Christian university in central Arkansas known for saying things like, "Turn to your right or left—that may be your spouse..." The emphasis on marriage and finding a spouse within a strong pool of possibilities made the term "marriage factory" a common descriptor for the university.

Many of the parents of those students, my own included, met in college and married. Following in their parents' footsteps, many young women had the goal and expectation of obtaining her "M.R.S." (a marriage license being a higher priority than a B.A., B.S. or other professional licensure).

Admonitions like, "It's easier to fish in a pool full of fishes," while true, can place undue added pressure on someone to find a spouse before one or the other is ready. If you didn't "catch a fish" before graduation, then you might feel that you were a failure.

That same intense pressure is not exclusive to Christian universities. Many church camps, campus ministries, or young professionals groups can intentionally or inadvertently create the same atmosphere. The perceived pressure is a combination of internal unmet desires and external contributing factors.

In any of the contexts mentioned above, I wish they would've said, "Turn to your right and your left, these are the Kingdom workers with whom you are building foundational relationships and life-long friendships. These are your future teammates in church plants and in missions, your kindred spirits in business and in service, as well as some of the Christian brothers and sisters with whom you will celebrate the joys of life and mourn its losses."

So, let's celebrate, mourn, and continue to converse together (Rom. 12:15). The spirit of this book is celebratory, not accusatory. We are facilitating a conversation and shedding light on a different perspective. We value the place that every member has in the body and every single person has in the Kingdom.

CHAPTER 3

The Church and Society

A kindergartener dons her miniature cap and gown, sings in the school program with her peers, and anticipates moving on to first grade. The elementary student transitions to middle school or junior high, wishing she could jump right into high school. Seventh grade is followed by eighth; eighth is followed by ninth, and soon graduation is around the corner.

Whether or not the student continues to college, additional expectations depend on the career path chosen or the limitations of those choices, determined by various internal and external factors.

Either way, the natural progression of schooling creates an anticipation of the next step forward. Across various cultural groups within the United States, even if no one has verbalized or formalized marriage expectations, the assumption is adopted by many an insecure teen, wishing and hoping for her own "happily ever after" story.

For someone like Jamie, a senior in college, singleness was never a part of the picture or the conversation until later.

I grew up having never met anyone that was single past the age of 30. It just wasn't a thing you saw in the church. Because of this, I went into college seeking attention from guys and putting my worth in whether I was in a relationship or not. My thought was always, "What does it say about you if no one wants to be in a relationship with you?" Then one day I walked into "singles chapel" and my thought process was truly changed. I saw these amazing women doing things for the Lord that they could have never done if they had a husband or families holding them back. **The freedom to follow God with reckless abandon was what really drew me to value my singleness.** Right now, being single, I am in a unique position to be able to do crazy things or go to outrageous places that God leads me to because I don't have any strings attached.

For most, singleness has not been normalized in their culture, vocabulary, nor relationships. The perpetuated expectation of marriage, the seemingly reasonable assumption of marriage until death, and the perceived judgement enforced upon anyone who does not follow those patterns lead to encaging traps like comparison that can hinder us from living out our one single reason: love. A deeper conversation about those traps and how to avoid them will take place in Section IV, but let's discuss first some of the social and societal factors that can encourage us to normalize singleness and bring its merits into our everyday conversations.

The average age for women to get married in 1950 was 20.3 years old. Each decade has seen a steady rise in the average age such that in 2019, the average age for women to marry was 28! (The average ages for men in 1950 and then in 2019 were 22.8 and 29.8, respectively.)[7]

---

[7] U.S. Census Bureau, Current Population Survey, March and Annual Social and Economic Supplements (2019).

The train that carried many people toward marriage has derailed as countless social factors contribute to a very different pattern or timetable than that of our parents or grandparents.

A discussion about the differences between the Silent Generation, Boomers, Gen Xers, Millennials, and Homelanders (Gen Z) could be beneficial to this conversation, so I encourage you to engage people of multiple generations in your dialogue.

Besides generational differences, some of the social or societal factors contributing to a higher average age for marriage are women in higher education and the workforce. Women have earned more bachelor's degrees than men since 1982, more master's degrees than men since 1987, and more doctorate degrees than men since 2006.[8]

The choice used to be between a career and a marriage. However, the glass ceiling has been lifted and what used to be an either/or choice has become more of an expectation of both/and. The percentage of women in the workforce has been a steady climb from 1948 until 1995 (28.6% to 46.1%), from which point it mostly has plateaued (46.8% in 2016).[9] This is still nearly half of all women over age 16.

Mere months before COVID-19 was officially declared a pandemic and created a severe impact on our global economy, there were more women in the U.S. workforce than men (50.04%; 109,000 more women). Economists quoted in Forbes.com in January 2020 affirmed that this trend will continue and that "women will increasingly dominate the labor market." Some of the primary contributing factors

---

[8] "Women in the Workforce-United States: Quick Take," Catalyst, 14 Oct 2020. https://www.catalyst.org/research/women-in-the-workforce-united-states/

[9] "Women in the Labor Force." U.S. Department of Labor, 2020. https://www.dol.gov/agencies/wb/data/facts-over-time/women-in-the-labor-force#civilian-labor-force-by-sex

were higher education and women occupying jobs that were once considered male-oriented.[10]

Elizabeth, a university professor who educates teachers, is a single woman, never married, who has invested in every student she has had the honor of teaching over the years. She provides insight on the implications and perceptions of her career path through an interview.

Sometimes I perceive that people view me as being younger or immature because I don't know what it's like to be married. I haven't fought those battles. I haven't lived those joys. And the same could be said with children. But the interesting thing that I think sometimes is forgotten is that, because of my specific profession, I have worked with children. And sometimes I have worked with children closely longer than a mother has been raising her child. So, there are insights and there are perspectives in loving and working with children that those people don't understand. It's just interesting. That's not a value judgement, it just can sometimes cause frustration for me because there's a lack of understanding. Or I feel as though I get treated like I don't know whenever there are some insights that I do have. Or the fact that I have chosen to follow God on this path for a life that has been more career minded. Sometimes from other women, there is a belittling because the focus of my life—what it's had to be, because that's what God has placed in front of me—is my career rather than to [focus on] a husband and children.

And unfortunately, in our faith background, being a wife and mother has been prioritized over... has been viewed to be more significant, or a better contribution to our world, than being good and contributing in meaningful ways in a profession and a career. I always know that it's not intentional, but it's still hard to swallow that sometimes.

Elizabeth's insights are revelatory. As she states in another part of her interview, sometimes a young woman simply continues moving

---

[10] Jack Kelly, "Women Now Hold More Jobs Than Men in the U.S. Workforce," *Forbes*, 13 Jan 2020. https://www.forbes.com/sites/jackkelly/2020/01/13/women-now-hold-more-jobs-than-men/?sh=2a928de68f8a

forward with her education and career, making the most of every opportunity. **What didn't start as a career-oriented pursuit became the best course of action when marriage was not an available option.**

And what about those single moms who would've preferred to stay home with their children, but for whom full-time work has also been a necessity? According to the Department of Labor's Women's Bureau, mothers are the primary or sole earners in 40 percent of households with children under age 18. In 1960, that number was only 11 percent.[11]

What does this mean for single and single-again women in our churches? And what about those who are not currently attending church?

Additional stats could be shared from the United States Census Bureau, Pew Research, the Department of Labor's Women's Bureau, and others. They each provide statistical insights into the population demographics and certain breakdowns of those populations in the U.S. Instead of filling this book with statistical perspectives, I prefer to highlight the stories of these women as representatives and facilitators of our larger conversation.

It is a worldwide challenge that we must make ourselves aware of and learn to navigate and normalize in our conversations. Sheritha, a single woman missionary in the Netherlands, summarizes,

> In Europe, they assume that single means dating, so many people in relationships avoid going to our Singles Retreat (I organize this with two others). Also, there seems to be a stigma, so people are afraid of going because they do not want to seem desperate. I think if churches

---

[11] "Women in the Labor Force." U.S. Department of Labor. https://www.dol.gov/agencies/wb/data/facts-over-time/women-in-the-labor-force#civilian-labor-force-by-sex as cited in Career Contessa, "11 Encouraging Statistics on Women in the Workplace," Career Contessa, 8 Mar 2019. https://www.careercontessa.com/advice/women-in-the-workplace-stats/

made it a normal thing to be single and spend time with each other to build each other up, people would be less afraid of sending the wrong message with getting involved in singles activities.

I love what Sheritha says about making it a normal thing to be single and spending time with each other to build each other up! We need the support and encouragement of one another, no matter what our season of life. Our support of one another is vital *"as each part does its work"* (Eph. 4:16, NIV).

The data shared and the stories told are intended to be descriptive and not prescriptive. **No matter our marital status, God can use any and every relationship to make us more holy.** I especially appreciate the premise of *Sacred Marriage* by Gary Thomas. His subtitle "What if God designed marriage to make us holy more than to make us happy?" reminds me of the blessing of iron sharpening iron relationships in my life that have certainly made me holy (Prov. 27:17).

CHAPTER 4

God's Word Has Not Changed

Affirmed by 1 Corinthians 12, God designed His body to have a variety of members. In His Kingdom, with Christ as the head, God has called for a diversity of members, celebrating different talents, marital statuses, stages of life, cultural and linguistic backgrounds.

With our diverse experiences and unique stories, we are all among the walking wounded of the Lord's army. I love the analogy that compares the church to a hospital. Yet, some of our wounds are more visible than those of others. Across the gospels, we see Jesus reach into the lives of people from all walks of life, suffering from a variety of ailments. He came to heal, and not just the physical ailments. As He affirmed in Luke 4, He came to fulfill the prophecy in Isaiah 61.

> *1 The Spirit of the Lord God is upon me,*
> *because the Lord has anointed me*
> *to bring good news to the poor;*
> *he has sent me to bind up the brokenhearted,*
> *to proclaim liberty to the captives...*
> *2 to comfort all who mourn.* (Is. 61:1, 2b, ESV)

Jesus sees the struggles that single and single-again women face. Through the brokenhearted moments, the mourning of expectations, and even the feeling of captivity while desiring to break free, Christ sees each of us. Whether singleness is a path that was deliberately chosen or not, the struggles and pain are real. My single sister, you are not alone.

Jesus was single. I have already mentioned Miriam, Nehemiah, Mary, Martha, and Paul, while neglecting the single-again like Ruth, Naomi, or Anna, and the single moms like Hagar. We will discuss each of these examples, but this list is far from exhaustive. Can we take the time to celebrate their singleness as part of their stories?

Single women, among other marginalized individuals, have a greater desire and heightened sensitivity to whether they see themselves identified or represented. A single, never married friend, Angela R. tells of her efforts to help others see and understand those who feel excluded.

I was part of a group discussion about ways in which we would like to see our church grow. I said that I would like to see the church become more fully inclusive of people on the margins of the congregation, such as single adults and African Americans. A married, white man replied, "I've never seen anyone on the margins here, and if they are, it's their own fault for not taking advantage of opportunities to get involved." This man somehow managed to simultaneously deny the reality of my struggle and blame me for it.

Thankfully, when I have observed married women engaging in meaningful conversation with single and single-again women (especially in a small group setting), most have responded to the feelings of exclusion with sincere remorse and gratefulness to be made aware of another's perspective. Additionally, many have offered sincere apologies, coupled with statements like, "It was never intentional."

Misunderstandings, assumptions, comparisons, expectations, and even judgements (on any side) can hinder our contentment and create a perceived divide that God never intended, but that Satan wants to capitalize on.

Drawing from negative experiences in our past, it can be easy to assume the worst of others. Our attempts to broach the subject of how singles may be feeling in the church have been met with resistance, so we get discouraged. It is still a worthwhile conversation, and we don't want Satan to win. God knows our desire to be understood and to have a voice, no matter our marital status. He will strengthen you and give you wisdom as you move forward in this conversation.

Prayerfully, we will either find the courage to speak up, or there will be someone else who bravely expresses a depth of understanding. As Dina, a single-again sister for 19 years said,

> I learned how to find my voice and reach out to other ladies who needed a word of encouragement or to speak up in class when there are generalities being stated as fact. I have found quite often that there are other ladies in the class who needed to feel like someone understood and, by my speaking up, they didn't feel so disconnected.

When we feel seen, heard, and understood, we often feel freer to engage in deeper conversations. **Our spiritual battles are similar, but the battleground is different.** Paul addressed this in 1 Corinthians 7. Both married and unmarried individuals were struggling to find contentment and to maintain their focus on the spiritual, instead of the sexual. Let's dig a little deeper into that text.

First Corinthians 7, the most referred to text regarding singleness, does not bash marriage; nor does it bash singleness. **The greater issue at hand was contentment in the life one has.** Allow me to lay the foundation of the biblical context of this chapter, a seminal passage in conversations on the topic of singleness.

Corinth was a wealthy port city. It is described as the vacation destination for many Romans in the prime of the Roman Empire. The Corinthians were so famous across the region for their pagan practices that a new term was adopted in Greek, "to corinthianize." "To live like a Corinthian" was characterized by drunkenness and sexual immorality. During the 1st century A.D., when Paul wrote his letters to the Corinthian church, he spoke to the influence of the immoral and highly sexualized culture, reminding them of the importance of obedience to Christ's teaching and clarifying the truths of that teaching.

When surrounded by a wide variety of philosophies, it can be hard to discern the truth. Corinth was a melting pot of many cultures and beliefs. One of the prominent practices of the time, stemming from the Greek and Roman influence, was to engage with the temple prostitutes. Venus was the Roman counterpart of the Greek goddess Aphrodite, both depicted as symbols of love, sex, beauty, fertility, and even prostitution. Their temple sat atop Acrocorinth, the mountain peak that overlooked Corinth, and was frequented by both men and women—locals, sailors, and other visitors.

Paul reminds the Corinthians who they should honor with their bodies.

[15] Do you not know that your bodies are members of Christ himself? Shall I then take the members of Christ and unite them with a prostitute? Never! [16] Do you not know that he who unites himself with a prostitute is one with her in body? For it is said, "The two will become one flesh." [17] But whoever is united with the Lord is one with him in spirit. [18] Flee from sexual immorality. All other sins a person commits are outside the body, but whoever sins sexually, sins against their own body. [19] Do you not know that your bodies are temples of the Holy Spirit, who is in you, whom you have received from God? You are not your own; [20] you were bought at a price. Therefore honor God with your bodies. (1 Cor. 6:15-20, NIV)

The next verse refers to an earlier letter Paul received from the Corinthians. In that letter, it appears that the teaching went to the other extreme, in reaction to the hypersexualized society: All sex is bad, even for married couples. *"It is good for a man not to have sexual relations with a woman"* (1 Cor. 7:1, NIV).

Paul clarifies throughout the seventh chapter of 1 Corinthians that sex has its proper place in marriage, but that, if you are able to remain pure, celibate, and fully dedicated to God, that is even better. Be content in the life you have (1 Cor. 7:17). **Don't let the desire for a different life steal the joy of your current calling.** Can we repeat that phrase, so it has a chance to sink in? Don't let the desire for a different life steal the joy of your current calling. Besides, in the following verses, Paul affirms that it is not necessarily a permanent state.

One of the most affirming truths for singles is found later in this chapter:

[32] I would like you to be free from concern. An unmarried man is concerned about the Lord's affairs—how he can please the Lord. [33] But a married man is concerned about the affairs of this world—how he can please his wife— [34] and his interests are divided. An unmarried woman or virgin is concerned about the Lord's affairs: Her aim is to be devoted to the Lord in both body and spirit. But a married woman is concerned about the affairs of this world— how she can please her husband. [35] I am saying this for your own good, not to

restrict you, but that you may live in a right way in undivided devotion to the
Lord. (1 Cor. 7:32-35, NIV)

Single women agree that we have heard very few sermons on this topic. Yes, there were the occasional youth group discussions when we broke into two groups by gender, but no one wanted to relive the direction those talks went. "Sex is bad." "Don't be a stumbling block for the young men by the way you dress." Statements intended as a warning served to misrepresent the truths laid out in Scripture.

From the pulpit, the general silence on sex and singleness illustrates the disconnect that many singles feel in this area. Then, when most applications and illustrations are drawn from the marriage relationship, where does a single woman find her understanding on these topics? And what about all the other "one-another" relationships in our lives?

Of note for our divorced or separated single-again sisters, a study of the text in Matthew 19 is most often focused on divorce's spiritual validity (or not). That is not what we are addressing in this book. I will leave it to biblical scholars to provide you with an exegetical study of the original meaning of that text. Theologians and hermeneutical scholars can help you apply that understanding to our modern-day context.

For our purposes, we prefer to focus on the support for that single-again woman rather than on the reasons behind any kind of separation. **The Scarlet D of divorce she feels that she wears does not serve as an invitation for us to shame the wounded.** Rather, we will avoid the trap of those judgements and other similar traps (Section IV), we will offer support (Section II), and we will walk with her as she navigates how to respond (Section V).

The traps, the need for support, and the challenges of knowing how to respond pertain to the never married, as well. There are more similarities than differences among single women, which will be illustrated by the women who share their stories. **I believe that all**

women will identify with the same struggles, just in a different context of life circumstances. Remember, it is often the same battle, just a different battleground.

Ladies, allow me one more story before we get into the practical steps we can take, moving forward in the conversation.

Fruit Basket Turnover

At weddings, when "all the single ladies" are called together in order for the bride to throw the bouquet, besides wanting the earth to swallow and hide me from the attention and emphasis placed on everyone's supposed desire to be "the next one to get married...," it reminds me of the game "Fruit Basket Turnover" and the middle-school awkwardness many single and single-again women describe.

Church camp, circa 1985: Sweaty middle schoolers are seated in a circle on metal folding chairs, swatting at mosquitos and secretly staring at their camp crush across the way. The counselors begin to explain the rules for the next game to be played: Fruit Basket Turnover.

"One person stands in the middle and calls out something like, 'Everyone wearing socks.' Then, everyone wearing socks must get up and find a different chair to go sit in. The person in the middle must also find a chair, but there will be someone left in the middle without a chair after everyone else has found a seat. It is then that person's turn to call something out."

The groans are audible, and while some kids are sitting at the edge of their chair, ready to run if the statement applies to them, others are sliding down in their chairs, wishing they could be invisible.

"Everyone born in March!" yells the counselor, and the scurrying begins. "Everyone wearing braces," states the next person to get caught in the middle—as if everyone in braces is not feeling obvious enough. "Anyone who is here for the first time..."

The game continues until the counselors suspect that some campers have not moved from their original seats. They then call out "Fruit Basket Turnover," and everyone must get up and find a new chair to sit in.

Feeling "singled out" in the game of life, women can get the same feeling in church. Those who do not have someone to sit with on Sunday morning can feel like the one left without a chair.

The rules have changed, but the game is the same. The awkwardness continues as people feel singled out by comments from the pulpit. How do we, as a church, present solid, biblical teaching on marriage without negating or ignoring our single members? If we never speak of the blessings, challenges, and biblical teaching about singleness, what is implied? When all of our language reflects marriage and family terminology, what else are we communicating?

I have observed in many places that the church elevates marriage to the point of idolizing it. Marriage can be a blessed, positive thing. It is compared to Christ's love for the church (Eph. 5:25). We want to honor marriage and support those who are married, but we do not want it to be put on such a pedestal that anyone who is not married cannot be elevated and celebrated on that same level.

The perception is created that women cannot fulfill God's purpose for their lives if they are not married and having children. As one woman expressed it, "It's like you're incomplete or insignificant without a spouse." Or, as another asked, "Why is being single seen as less than being married?"

Whether single or single-again, respondents to the survey perceive significant disapproval and a projected feeling of incompleteness, especially from older church members.

"You aren't living up to your potential."

"Are you even dating someone?"

"If you don't hurry up, you won't be able to have children…"

"Whose fault was it that your marriage failed?"

"Aren't you lonely?"

Are you bristling with me at the sting of those remarks? We all can do better!

Besides, rare is the couple who marries young and dies simultaneously as his/her spouse after many years of marriage. No matter the age at which someone marries, before and after their marriage, the bride and groom were each single. Therefore, we must recognize that **every individual will be single for one or more times in life**.

So, how can we support each other as single or single-again individuals, especially women?

SECTION I

Table Talk

After a discussion of this first section during a pilot study of this material, Sydney, a senior in college, texted me afterward,

At some point, every woman in this room has had some type of experience where they weren't invited to the table, and tonight was an invitation for us all to have a seat. I have never witnessed a more humble community of women gathered together by such an invitation as this.

Amen! That is my prayer as you continue these conversations and extend these invitations.

Each section will conclude with the following segments: Talk with God (Reflection Questions), Talk with an Iron Rose Sister (Common Threads), Table Talk with One Another, and Walk the Talk.

Talk with God (Reflection Questions)

What are your initial takeaways from this section?

Why is singleness an important topic to address? Name three people with whom you would like to have this conversation.

The statement was made, "I have observed in many places that the church elevates marriage to the point of idolizing it." Do you agree or disagree? How so or why not?

Talk with an Iron Rose Sister

 The **Common Threads** are found in all Iron Rose Sister Ministries Small Group Bible Studies.[12] They are a way to make any lesson personal and practical and are taken from the three parts of the ministry's logo.

An area in which you want to grow or bloom

---

[12] For more information about Iron Rose Sister Ministries, our small group Bible study materials, and other resources, including additional resources for facilitating this conversation with single women and church leaders, see Chapter 34, "About Iron Rose Sister Ministries," and visit our website, https://IronRoseSister.com/.

A thorn you'd like to remove (a hindrance from moving forward in this conversation)

An area in which you'd like to dig deeper or need someone to hold you accountable

Ideally, the Common Threads are shared with at least one other person in order that we can serve as iron sharpening iron (Prov. 27:17), encouraging each other to be as beautiful as a rose, in spite of a few thorns.

Table Talk with One Another (one-on-one or group discussion)

Tell me something about your story. What makes you uniquely you?

How has the topic of singleness impacted you? What makes this conversation important to you?

How have you seen social media influence your feelings and perceptions about singleness?

Can you describe for me an experience in which you felt like you didn't have a seat at the table or a voice in the conversation? What are some concrete suggestions that we can each take to help avoid this from happening to others in the future?

What insights were gleaned about 1 Corinthians 7, after the description of the Corinthian culture?

What is your reaction to the contents of this first section? What has contributed to your reaction? As you dialogue about this, be sure to listen, learn, and love each other.

How have your insights or perceptions changed after discussing aspects of this first section with someone else?

Walk the Talk

What is one single **Action Step** you can take? Describe some next level conversations to have with others.

Tips for Small Group Table Talk

We want to set the table, spiritually speaking, and prayerfully prepare for everyone to love, listen, and learn. Everyone comes to the table with different perspectives and expectations for this discussion.

Welcome every single person (aka, everyone!) to the table.

When gathering or recruiting a group of people to discuss this together, the more diverse the women, the richer the experience, even though it may come with initial challenges of learning how each person communicates.

Remember our one single reason and trust the process. God's got this! And He is thrilled to lead you through this ongoing conversation.

Section II

Supporting One Another
(Offer a PEAR)

Let each of you look not only to his own interests,
but also to the interests of others. (Phil. 2:4, ESV)

Sometimes, the language we used to describe someone unintentionally demonstrates a lack of support. The term "your other half" when someone refers to his/her spouse is sweet when we think about how the two become one, but does that imply that a single person is incomplete without that other half?

One is a whole number whether it is a single person or the "one" that the two become when they are married (Eph. 5:31; Gen. 2:24). I know the math doesn't work out logically, but, in Spanish, the language on this topic can be even more frustrating: "The other half of your orange."

Señoritas (single women) must always be ready to answer where the other half of her orange is. (¿Dónde está tu media naranja?) The implication of incompleteness in that cultural expression is even more glaring than in English.

As an alternative to the fruity Spanish expression of finding the other half of your orange, I would like to propose that we offer each other a different type of fruit—one that is not based on being half of a whole or being "paired" with anyone, but rather a **PEAR: Prayer, Encouragement, Activities, and Reminders of Truth.**

Like the young señorita who is constantly being asked where the other half of her orange is, a single woman may not fully realize her completeness in Christ. The distracted nature of the world we live in can make it more challenging for all of us to keep our relationship with God at the forefront. Therefore, we pray and we support each other through Prayer, the first part of the PEAR.

CHAPTER 5

Prayer

At a birthday party, it came time to serve the cake.
A little boy named Brian blurted out, "I want the biggest piece!"
His mother quickly scolded him.
"Brian, it's not polite to ask for the biggest piece."
The little guy looked at her in confusion, and asked,
"Well then, how do you get it?"[13]

We often want to fix someone else's problem, to take away her pain, or even request the biggest piece of cake on her behalf, but many times the *only* thing we can do is the *best* thing we can do: pray. When we let someone know we are praying for them, we affirm three significant truths. These three affirmations of support are, **"You are loved. You are prayed for. And you are not alone."**

Satan wants to isolate us. Single and single-again women often are already feeling isolated, ostracized, and alienated. The encouragement and support we can offer one another through prayer are key to feeling heard, valued, and included.

---

[13] Olive Freeman in Edward K. Rowell and *Leadership*, editors. *1001 Quotes, Illustrations, and Humorous Stories for Preachers, Teachers, and Writers.* (Grand Rapids, Michigan: Baker Books. 2008), 331

Paul mentions throughout the epistles the strength he gleans from the prayers of others. And his constant prayers for the ones to whom he writes are an evidence of his love for them and the joy with which he remembers them in his prayers (Phil. 1:3-11).

One of my favorite prayers of Paul's is especially appropriate to be prayed over each other as single women. The truths in Ephesians 3:14-21 speak light into the darkness and power into the weakness. I encourage you to insert a single woman's name into the prayer as you intercede on her behalf. (I have given you a sample below using my own name.)

¹⁴ For this reason [out of love for my single friend], I kneel before the Father, ¹⁵ from whom every family in heaven and on earth derives its name. ¹⁶ I pray that out of His glorious riches He may strengthen [Michelle] with power through His Spirit in [her] inner being, ¹⁷ so that Christ may dwell in [Michelle's] heart through faith. And I pray that [Michelle], being rooted and established in love, ¹⁸ may have power, together with all the Lord's holy people, to grasp how wide and long and high and deep is the love of Christ, ¹⁹ and to know this love that surpasses knowledge—that [Michelle] may be filled to the measure of all the fullness of God.

²⁰ Now to Him who is able to do immeasurably more than all we ask or imagine, according to His power that is at work within us, ²¹ to Him be glory in the church and in Christ Jesus throughout all generations, for ever and ever! Amen. (Eph. 3:14-21, NIV, adapted)

Sometimes it can be easier to pray for others than for yourself. If you need to read this prayer to yourself first, inserting your own name, go ahead! Aren't those powerful words? Yes, God loves YOU that much!

While Paul's examples of prayer are beautiful, the best examples of prayer come from Christ Himself. Jesus taught His disciples to pray (Matt. 6:5-15) and invited them to pray with Him (Luke 9:28). Jesus asked for prayers from His disciples on His behalf (Matt. 26:36-40) and He prayed on their behalf (John 17). In order to keep His focus and maintain His relationship with His Father, Jesus would often take some time away from others and pray (Matt. 14:23; Luke 5:16). On at least one occasion, He spent all night in prayer (Luke 6:12).

And why did Jesus pray on all these occasions? His one single reason: Love—for His Father and for every single one of us.

Drawing from Jesus' and Paul's examples, what are some of the benefits and blessings of prayer?

Secondly, what about prayer is supportive of others?

Prayer is fellowship. Prayer connects us with God and with one another on a deeper level than any other form of communication. There is a powerful, humbling vulnerability when we go to God on someone else's behalf or when we pray together aloud. When you express to someone that you are petitioning God on her behalf, she feels cared for and seen. You are standing in the gap for her with intentionality and sincerity (Rom 15:30).

Bonnie remembers exactly where she was standing when the preacher told her that he stands with her in the gap, that he goes before the throne of God on her behalf. He has reminded her of that truth on other occasions, as well. As a single woman, never married, in her late 30's, when Bonnie struggles with feelings of loneliness, she remembers the preacher's prayerful blessing and knows she is not alone.

We do not need to be preachers to stand in the gap with others and partner in prayer with them. Prayer is communion with God and with one another. Who can you fellowship with in prayer today?

Prayer maintains our focus. Whether we are asking for wisdom (James 1:5) or patience in affliction (Rom. 12:12), we can be faithful in prayer bringing others and ourselves before God (1 Tim. 2:1; 2 Tim. 1:3).

When we look to Him, He fills us with faith, love, hope, strength, and the same power that raised His Son from the dead (Eph. 1:15-20)!

One single sister, in the context of a Bible study small group, shared, "When a sister in Christ asks me about something specific that we have prayed about together in the past, I am so encouraged. It shows me that I am important enough to her and to God for her to bring my request before our Heavenly Father. It also reminds me that God is the one who can truly make a difference in that situation. Instead of stressing about it, it reminds me to ask myself if I have prayed about it."

Prayer provides deep connection through shared burdens. Liliana loves to tell other single women about the depth of relationship formed with her prayer partners as they pray over their shared struggles together, as single women.

Katie F., echoing the sentiments of James 5:13-18, says, "I've never regretted pausing to pray for someone in the moment. Sometimes it is a silent prayer. And sometimes I stop in the middle of wherever we are and say a prayer for her, out loud, for her to hear the burden that is now shared being lifted to God. Yeah, I have never regretted it."

Prayer gives it all over to God. The prayer of the persistent widow in Luke 18 demonstrates that it is most important to go to the one who has the power to do something about your circumstances. We cannot handle it on our own and should not even try.

I love how many people partnered in prayer with one single mom, all striving together to give the situation over to God along every challenging step of the way.

Two years earlier, when entering that same courtroom for the first time, the room felt large and everything loomed, including the anticipation of the rulings to be made. Burdened by the effects of sin not her own, she was reaping the consequences of her ex-husband's decisions. However, on the day of the custody trial, the room felt softer, smaller, even cozy. The difference? The cloud of witnesses that filled the courtroom.

Among those witnesses were the dozen or so who were sworn in before the judge. The forty plus people who trickled in and out during the nine-hour trial were prayer warriors and witnesses to God's faithfulness. The final group among the cloud of witnesses were the angels fighting in the spiritual battle and softening the cold, daunting nature of the proceedings.

God was glorified. And the greater testimony given for the judge, attorneys, bailiff, and others was not related specifically to the case, but rather to the testimony of how many of her Christian family showed up in physical presence compared to the void of people on his side of the courtroom. The one who showed up big-time, and even showed off, was God who received all the honor and praise for what happened that day.

For a single mom whose life had been turned upside down, she felt affirmed repeatedly that she was never alone. The physical presence of the witnesses... The thousands of prayers being lifted up on her behalf and on behalf of her daughter—even the prayers for her ex-husband to repent... The encouraging messages sent through the private Facebook group in which she sent updates with more specific prayer requests and expressions of praise and thankfulness... Love for God and love for a broken family was the cloud of witnesses' one single reason to show up that day.

This testimony of support is one small example of the power of prayer and the strength of its encouragement to a single or single-again woman (2 Cor. 1:11).

How have you been supported through prayer as a single woman? And how can you offer that prayerful support to others?

CHAPTER 6

Encouragement

W e all need a cheerleader, a Barnabas, a champion in our corner. While the women who participated in the survey did not specify who made the following comments, we can each see the value of these examples of encouragement.

Some affirmations were based on who they are as a person no matter where they found themselves in life at that point.

"You got this." "You're doing such an amazing job." "You've helped me." "You can do it!" "Your strength inspires and is noticed." "You are an example to so many people." "You were one of God's best ideas." "Your hands are like the hands of God reaching out to touch people."

And, for some, it was more specific to their current situation:

"It's an amazing honor to serve the Lord, no less honorable than being married."

"I am proud of what you have accomplished since your divorce."

"I am so glad that you are no longer living with your ex-husband's abuse."

One of the other sources of encouragement came from married women who spoke well of their own single years and allowed single women to be content in their own singleness.

"It's wonderful what God can teach you during this time of your life. I remember..."

"You really have a great life, just as it is!"

"That's really awesome that you are so content."

And for single moms, celebrating their children is always a plus!

"You are strong, and a great mom, and your daughter is blessed to have you."

"I love when I see my children's artwork on a friend's fridge or when someone comes up to my son and tells him how glad he is to see him at church."

Because of the nature of the surveys, I was not privileged to learn of the context of each of the quoted comments. **Please do not consider these comments to be a scripted list of what to or not to say.** It can be hard to know how someone will react to any statement being made. However, there are two things I can say definitively: 1) Prayer is our best tool to know whether to say something and what to say if and when we do. Ask God for discernment regarding whether or not your words will be received as an encouragement or discouragement. 2) No "one and done" statement is as powerful as an open dialogue that allows both sides to share feedback and mutual encouragement.

Because of the relational nature of her suggestion, I will share one more specific comment by Eve, a divorced, single mom, which affirms that words of encouragement are not the only ways to encourage and support single and single-again women. Note: This suggestion is for single or married individuals...

Adopt a single mom and her children as you would do for a niece in your family. Invite her as part of your family for lunch, take her kids to school or pick up after school, teach them to bake cookies, or help with homework. Hang their drawing on your fridge so they see you value them when they come over. Invite a single mom for coffee so she can have a time to vent (no need to fix anything, sometimes we just need to talk it out like a married woman would talk to her hubby at the end of the day). Come to her house and help her clean things up WITHOUT comment or judgement! Compliment her often, tell her children good things about their mom, tell her good things about her children.

As a single woman never married, one of the best encouragements I personally have received was in the form of advice that I have often repeated to myself and to other single women. As a visual learner, this illustration based on Hebrews 12:1-2; 1 Corinthians 9:24-27; 2 Corinthians 6:14, and other passages, has been especially helpful.

*¹ Therefore, since we are surrounded by so great a cloud of witnesses, let us also lay aside every weight, and sin which clings so closely, and **let us run with endurance the race that is set before us,** ² looking to Jesus, the founder and perfecter of our faith, who for the joy that was set before him endured the cross, despising the shame, and is seated at the right hand of the throne of God. (Heb. 12:1-2, ESV, emphasis added)*

Run to God. Keep your eyes fixed on Him. If, as you run along, you find someone else running to God and you both decide to keep running toward God together, for the rest of your lives, awesome! However, if you sit on the sidelines and wait for an awesome Christian guy to run by, then you start to get up and run to catch up with him, you will be out of shape and you will never make it to your goal. What is your goal anyway? To seek God or to find a man? Conversely, if you are running to God and see some guy sitting out of the race, someone who is not keeping his own eyes fixed on the goal, then that is not the kind of guy you want to make your life partner.

For those women who are single-again, I am sorry for the loss of the one you thought was going to be your life partner. For the separated or divorced, no matter the reason, I pray for strength and perseverance as you continue to run the race. And for the single moms, there are others of us cheering you and your children on toward the goal for which we have all been called heavenward (Phil. 3:12-14).

I celebrate the mothers who strive diligently to protect their children from the challenges and negativity that are natural byproducts of divorce. For those who had abusive husbands, I applaud you for choosing safety and health over the damaging effects of long-term abuse.

For every single one of us, no matter our circumstances, God wants what is best for us as His beloved daughters (Songs 2:4; Eph. 3:3-14). Therefore, no matter what place you find yourself in life, let's live out Romans 12:15 together. Let's celebrate. Let's grieve. And let's run!

Let's Celebrate!

I love being "the fun aunt." I have treated many of my friends' children as my nieces and nephews. Celebrating their birthdays, their accomplishments, and listening to their struggles is important, especially in support of single moms. As a church, we recognize that an emphasis on the family unit can leave the single woman, never married, and the single-again sister feeling less supported and less celebrated. We're in this together, ladies! And we have a tremendous opportunity to celebrate one another as church family, whether the families we grew up in are nearby or far away.

Thankfully, that spirit of adoption and celebration was one I grew up seeing modeled at our dining room table with my parents. They included single moms and single women into our extended family, especially at holiday times. My continuation of that practice has included a few fun activities I will mention later in this section, but the encouragement given and received by including one another into each other's families applies to us single women, as well. Does your table have a spot for a few more?

Susan: I think it is also important as a single person to recognize my role in that I cannot expect or assume that somebody is going to come alongside me and be those support systems. It is also my responsibility to walk alongside other people, whether that be as a mentor to someone else, or if it is being mentored by someone else who has more life experience than I do. It's a two-way street.

And when we take part in the one-another nature of our Christian family relationships, we can better encourage one another in the times of rejoicing.

> Susan later continues, "We often celebrate major milestones of life that are associated with marriage... engagement parties, weddings, wedding showers, baby showers, gender reveals, new home pantry stockings... And those are wonderful things to celebrate! But for an individual like me, most of those events I have not experienced, and therefore, throughout my adult life I have not felt very celebrated in most congregations I have been a part of."

Susan's suggestion is that we **celebrate momentous events and major accomplishments** that are comparable for a single person: graduating with an advanced degree, purchasing a first home, a significant new job, choosing to serve as a single missionary... any major life event that can be celebrated should be, whether they are significant for married or single individuals.

What can you celebrate with someone this week?

Let's Grieve

On the flip side of the celebration coin is grief. *"Rejoice with those who rejoice; mourn with those who mourn"* (Rom. 12:15, NIV).

Death is not the only source of grief. In a later section I will discuss the concept of "mourning expectations," but for now, suffice it to say that any sort of loss—a relationship, a dream, or a death—takes us through the five stages of grief.

A "puppy love" breakup between teenagers may cause us to roll our eyes and shake our heads. Nevertheless, a seasoned youth minister once reminded me, "It matters to the puppy." Our levels of loss are not a competition, nor should we fall into the trap of comparison. Grief is grief, and loss is loss. We are not to judge those facing a time of mourning. Rather, we are invited to mourn with them.

The single, never married, young woman who is thrilled for her third friend in a row to get engaged may also be grieving that she won't be the fourth in that line. She likely won't open up about that on a Sunday morning after the announcement, but a consistent conversation and genuine friendship may allow her the opportunity to share her conflicting emotions in a safe space with another Christian sister.

Considering its destructive nature, we all wish that divorce could be avoided. However, we will leave the preventative discussion to another day because, which is more important? To understand every aspect of what is going on in order to determine whether we approve or not, or support a broken person who has lost most aspects of the life she thought she was going to have? Our focus is to address the ways to support those who find themselves in the unfortunate circumstances of a separation or divorce.

The single-again woman is grieving. Whether she is going through a separation, a divorce, or the death of a spouse, she needs our support (for more time and in more ways than most realize). How can we encourage those who are grieving? Our words will be insufficient initially, but a simple card in the mail, a meal left on the doorstep, a gentle hug, a seat next to you at church, an invitation for coffee... are all great steps toward showing the love of God and the love of others. There may not be an official meal train for "divorce casseroles," but we can individually find ways to support and encourage our single-again sisters during a difficult time.

Name a single or single-again sister you know who is currently in need of support through grief. (Feel free to write down only her initials out of respect for what is possibly the private nature of her grief.)

And Let's Run!

Returning to our Hebrews 12 analogy and the race we are running toward God... Running to God is the best way to pursue our one single reason of love. When I run to God, I lose the labels and keep my focus. When I run to God, my love for Him grows. And when I encourage others, my love for them grows.

Through this book, we are developing a larger cloud of witnesses cheering us on toward the goal. **We are gaining cheerleaders and supportive Christian sisters.** No matter what our stage in life or marital status, everyone gets a little weary on the journey of doing good (Gal. 6:9). How can we encourage one another and spur each other on to love and good deeds (Heb. 10:24-25)? By getting together!

Miriam, one of God's single servants, was there walking with the Israelites out of Egypt and through the desert, with Pharaoh and his men on their heels. After passing through the Red Sea on dry land, she led the women to celebrate God's faithfulness (Ex. 15:20-21, ESV).

> *[21] And Miriam sang to them: "Sing to the Lord, for he has triumphed gloriously; the horse and his rider he has thrown into the sea."*

I met a mom in her neighborhood on Friday mornings before work so that we could walk (not run!), talk, and pray together. Her kids were old enough to get on the bus before school, then she had 20 minutes before she needed to leave for work. Those twenty minutes became a lifeline for both of us and an encouragement to keep running the race and keep fixing our eyes on Jesus—because we were not "running" alone.

Let's celebrate, let's grieve, and let's run... together!

> *[5] May the God of endurance and encouragement grant you to live in such harmony with one another, in accord with Christ Jesus, [6] that together you may with one voice glorify the God and Father of our Lord Jesus*

Christ. ⁷Therefore welcome one another as Christ has welcomed you, for the glory of God. (Rom. 15:5-7, ESV)

CHAPTER 7

Activities

And whatever you do, in word or deed, do everything in the name of the Lord Jesus, giving thanks to God the Father through him. (Col. 3:17, ESV)

A ctivities for the sake of activity or busy-ness are not healthy. Purposeful activities have the capacity to act as a catalyst for relationship. **Activities for the sake of relationship are at the heart of how we can support one another through this facet of offering a PEAR: Activities.**

Responses to survey questions were mixed about whether separate activities, events, or groups for singles or for women would best meet a single woman's needs. As noted in some of the answers, one alternative presented was intergenerational or diverse gatherings of the church community since one of the challenges in modern American churches is the segregation of classes by life stage. After graduating from the youth group to the campus ministry, if you are not married, where do you go next?

Although we will address some facets of the activity-type suggestions more specifically in Section VI: Congregational

Strategies, one significant note was that **all the activity-related answers expressed a common desire for connection.** For example, "Be truly interested in how they are doing... Really get to know the single people in your church" (71-year-old divorcee). **One-on-one relationships are much more meaningful than corporate-level programs.**

Sometimes, the relationship is formed by a simple, **"Want to join me?"** as an invitation to an already-established activity. A church picnic is being planned... Your small group is hosting a potluck... The Children's Ministry is recruiting new teachers... You're headed to a Bible class or are thinking about checking out the ladies' class... "Want to join me?"

> Jessica: Individually reaching out to women who may be hesitant to go to a small group or participate in a ministry that more naturally attracts couples/families or something they may not want to go to alone.

A couple of single girlfriends thought the announced topic for a ladies' day sounded fun, but knew that it often was catered more to married women than singles. Instead of avoiding the event, they decided to go together and remind others of their presence in the congregation. They determined ahead of time that they were going to have a great time and learn together, even challenging each other to make the extra effort to meet at least one other woman before the day was over.

On the flip side, **"May I join you?"** is another excellent question. A young student is sitting by herself on a Sunday morning... A visitor is quietly stirring her coffee, awkwardly looking around the room for someone she knows... A recently separated sister is sitting on the back pew, hoping to avoid the question-filled stares... everyone feels left out at one time or another.

Asking, "May I join you?" invites other women to be a part. Invite yourself to sit with single women. Help them feel included. If you have ever felt like the black sheep of the family, I can assure you that there are other women, not just singles, who likely have felt the same way. May we each remember that Jesus left the 99 to go and find the one (Luke 15:3-7).

The intentionality with which Jesus treated others affirmed that every single individual was seen and loved. He always knew His one single reason. And He was not afraid to create an activity in the other person's house, simply as an excuse to hang out with them. Remember when He invited Himself over to Zacchaeus' (Luke 19)?

Asking questions and spending time together are the best ways to get to know one another and deepen relationships.

Activities outside of the congregational context are an excellent source of support for each other. "Want to grab coffee sometime?" "We work not too far from each other. Want to meet for lunch sometime?" It does not have to be anything formal, nor does it have to be a special occasion.

One of the most memorable activities among two single women, a single mom, and her young daughter was a "Girls Night" that turned into an "Un-birthday party." The hostess made dinner and provided games. The single mom brought her and her daughter's favorite colors of fingernail polish to add to the hostess' overabundance of red-only options (yes, I was the hostess). And the other single girl brought dessert to share. Full from dinner, the ladies decided that dessert could wait until after they had played at least one game. But once the daughter saw the chocolate cake, that was it. It was time for dessert.

"Whose birthday is it?" asked the inquisitive six-year-old.

Her mom replied, "It's no one's birthday. Rosa just decided to bring a chocolate cake to share. Does it have to be someone's birthday for us to eat cake?"

"I hope not, because we all want cake!" I interjected. "But I do have candles and we could sing if you want."

My "niece" looked at me with a funny expression and finally asked, "But if it's no one's birthday, why would we put candles on the cake and sing Happy Birthday?"

"Have you ever watched the old Disney movie *Alice in Wonderland* or heard of the Very Merry Un-birthday song?"

After rolling her eyes, she looked to her mom to see if I was being serious or not. Undaunted by her skepticism, I opened my phone and pulled up a video from the movie which I blasted on full volume for an impromptu sing-off in my kitchen.

We all laughed as I got out teacups to accompany our cake. Then I lit the candles, and we sang "Happy Birthday to Nobody," all blowing out the candles together.

It may take extra effort to carve out time in our busy calendars, but no special occasion is needed to plan an activity together. And remember—the impromptu ones are often the most fun for building memories and lasting relationships!

If we depend solely on the activities organized by the church, we will find ourselves severely lacking in the depth of our one-another relationships. **Most of the one-another passages in Scripture cannot be fulfilled sitting shoulder to shoulder on Sunday mornings. They are best lived out in the time between those corporate gatherings through relationship.**

COVID-19 has reminded us of the advantages and disadvantages of our Sunday morning gatherings. However, the virus has also afforded many single women the opportunity to find new creative ways to serve.

Naomi, the children's librarian at her local church, started a Facebook page in which she posted clues for a Bible scavenger hunt on Tuesdays and a Bible trivia game on Fridays.

A group of recent college graduates shared a Google Slides document in which they created a "Corona Scrapbook." It included pictures of what they were doing, encouraging Bible verses, specific questions based on others' interests (e.g. What are you cooking?), and discussion pages on relevant real-word topics and personal struggles.

Ladies, these two examples of how we can encourage each other through Activities are amongst ourselves as single women during COVID-19. Guess what? We aren't the only ones with the "one single reason" of love. As the body of Christ, many of the married women and families also have this motivation and have lived out the truths of the following three summary statements, truly supporting one another and fulfilling our one single reason.

Through the results of the survey, when asked how single and single-again women would best feel supported, three key points rose to the surface. These statements, fleshed out below through stories and quotes, are also affirmed through the next section: Identifying the Deepest Desires of our Heart.

- Single women are not a project. We are people.
- Singleness is not a problem to be fixed.
- We are all vital members of the body. We need each other.

Do you agree with those three positions? What stories do you have to share that affirm or discredit these statements?

Single women are not a project. We are people.

When the family first "adopted me" as a single woman, relatively new to the congregation, there was no formal adoption ceremony nor any fanfare. What started as a lengthy conversation in the middle of the quiet neighborhood street after a ladies' Bible study became a life-long friendship. I may have invited myself to the first of their daughter's soccer games, but dinner at their house or mine became a regular occurrence.

Coffee with my friend was about two women getting together, encouraging each other in our Christian walks, sharing in the victories and challenges we each faced. Sometimes we would talk about her kids, or she would roll her eyes about a recent frustration with her husband. We would talk about my dreams of being a mom, how I "mothered" the students at our church, and "didn't have the pantry of a single person" (one of the best compliments her husband ever paid me).

This family that included me in their own meant that my grandma's cookie recipe, while not shared with my own children, became a tradition with their kids. The first time we took a road trip together, the kids wanted to ride with "the fun lady." The relationships we built when the kids were young made me a safe person with whom to have other conversations when they got a little older. It is important to have an "aunt" who will affirm what the parents are saying, but isn't mom or dad saying it.

One more story from that family: Living in Louisiana at the time, it was always important to spray your house for roaches and other pesky critters. So, when the dad mixed up the solution to spray their own house, he always mixed up a little bit more and came to spray mine too. Until he reads this, he may never know how much that meant to me. We were family and always will be.

> Angela B.: Invite and include them in activities, especially ones that are intergenerational and include families. [Singles] don't have a family at home, but they may want and need a family and can often feel excluded by so many things in the church that are family-oriented, whether it's intentionally family-oriented or not.

A single-again mom was feeling especially lonely once the pandemic hit and quarantine dragged on. She especially missed the Sunday morning fellowship, having to watch the online service by herself. When she expressed her feelings to her ladies' small group via Zoom, one sister printed out the faces of everyone in the small group and dropped them off at her doorstep. Everyone rejoiced at the picture of the table full of smiling faces taped to the backs of her chairs the following Sunday morning.

Singleness is not a problem to be fixed.

I have lost count of the times I have heard a mom, grandmother, aunt, or sister tell me that I would be just perfect for their son, grandson, nephew, or brother.

"I would love to fix y'all up."

"You just *have* to meet him."

And one of my all-time favorites, usually accompanied by a gentle touch of my hand, "You are exactly what he needs." I learned to respond to that last one with, "That's quite possible, but I'm not sure he's what I need."

The sentiment from these well-intentioned matchmakers felt the same no matter the specific wording of the offer: You are incomplete without a man in your life. You are a problem that needs to be fixed. I cannot comprehend that you might be content as a single woman.

Some single women reading this are nodding and laughing as they add to the list of goodhearted people's comments. Other single women are wishing they could hear some of those comments because the prospects in their local congregation or from the most-recently-attempted dating app are meager, at best.

How can we know the difference between what any two single women feel on this topic? You guessed it: relationship.

We are all vital members of the body. We need each other.

Angela R.: Often the modern American church has placed an extreme emphasis on marriage and the nuclear family. As a single woman, this leaves me struggling to find my place in the church. As a Marriage and Family Therapist, this emphasis worries me for the sake of our couples and families. People need community, and the Bible talks about church as a family, rather than emphasizing individual nuclear families. **The current over-emphasis on marriage and family often comes at the cost of the larger community.** That puts way too much pressure on marriages to meet needs that they were never intended to meet. Also, as of 2016, half of the adult American population was single. If the church is going to survive, it needs to find a place for people who don't have traditional families.

The one-another relationships in the body of Christ allow us to live out love through the intentionality of intimacy. In the same way that marriage allows for iron sharpening iron between spouses, relationships within the church also afford us the opportunity to be iron sharpening iron—an especially high priority for our Iron Rose Sister relationships. Marriage is not the only relationship designed with the higher priority of our holiness over our happiness. If we don't return to the relational truths as God explains them through Scripture, we will lose the benefit of those relationships formed in His name.

The concept of Church Family as Community and additional insights about Activities will be brought to the table of the conversation in Section VI: Congregational Strategies. In the meantime, let's look at one more way of Supporting One Another.

CHAPTER 8

Reminders of Truth

"The Bible is alive, it speaks to me; it has feet, it runs after me; it has hands, it lays hold of me." ~Martin Luther[14]

The last of the four ways in which we can support one another by offering a PEAR is Reminders of Truth. When I was in college, there was a particular guy who, deep down, I knew was not good for me. Yet he was easy to fall for and I constantly found myself pining for him. One day, as I confessed my desires to a friend she quickly responded, "That guy? But he's a jerk! Do you not remember when he...?" and she proceeded to remind me of his most annoying traits, less than gentlemanly behavior, and un-Christ-like attitude. "You deserve better than that! That is not the kind of guy God would want you to be with. It is not your job to save him or make him a better person. Do you hear me?"

I did hear her. And as painful as it seemed at the time, I knew she was right. I was too close to the situation and to him, to see the truth clearly. **The best way she could support me was to help me remember**

---

[14] Edward K. Rowell and *Leadership*, editors. *1001 Quotes, Illustrations, and Humorous Stories for Preachers, Teachers, and Writers*. (Grand Rapids, Michigan: Baker Books. 2008), 17

the truth that I had forgotten when I stumbled. I had lost sight of what was most important and needed a reminder, like we all do.

On more than one occasion, during my last two years of college, I would go back to her and say, "Can you remind me again why I shouldn't be with this guy? I don't know if I'm forgetful or if I just lose sight of the truth when I run into him on campus." She graciously, and sometimes very directly, would remind me of the truth. And her one single reason to do so? Love.

> [12] So I will always remind you of these things, even though you know them and are firmly established in the truth you now have. [13] I think it is right to refresh your memory as long as I live in the tent of this body,
> (2 Pet. 1:12-13, NIV)

My memory has needed a lot of refreshing when it comes to the topic of singleness. "Love is blind" has its advantages and its disadvantages. I am grateful for the "Peters" in my life who know that we need these reminders of truth.

I have already alluded to Satan's lies and the entrapping nature of his snares. However, if we do not recognize those lies, we will not be able to replace them with truth. In Matthew 12:43-45, when the evil spirit returned to the clean house and found it empty, he returned with seven other spirits more wicked than itself. **If we are going to recognize the lie and remove it, we must replace it with the truth.** Finally, even if we think we know that truth, we must remember the truth through a specific scripture.

Jesus taught us through His temptation that the best way to silence Satan is with the Bible (Luke 4:1-13). David also hid God's Word in his heart (Ps. 37:31; 119:11), one of the qualities that enabled him to be a man after God's own heart (1 Sam. 13:14; Acts 13:22).

In one of my other books, *Who Has the Last Word? Cutting through Satan's Lies with the Truth of God's Word*, I introduce a Lie/Truth Chart (also pictured here, pgs. 60-62). Several of the specific lies, each addressed in a separate chapter of that book, are extremely relevant to this conversation: "I am alone," "I am not enough," "I have to do it on my own," "Sexual lies," and "God is punishing me for my past." All lies! We will not address all of those lies here in this chapter, but I do want to introduce you to this tool that guides us to the reminders of truth in God's Word.

Using the chart below, beginning on the left, we write out a lie in our own words. To RECOGNIZE the lie is to bring it to light, stripping it of its power over us. Yet, if we do not REPLACE that lie with truth, we are doomed to fall back into the lie. The truth in the REPLACE column is also written out in our own words. Finally, the REMEMBER column highlights and reinforces that same truth in God's words.

The first three rows have all the blanks filled in so that you can familiarize yourself with this tool for remembering the truth. Rows 4-8 have various blanks so that you can begin to practice using this instrument by filling in the truths from the Bible, and also writing out a truth in your own words. Row 9 is left completely blank for you to write in your own lie. Below the chart is a list of helpful verses that can be used to fill in scriptures for rows 4-8.

RECOGNIZE the lie (in your own words)	REPLACE the lie with truth (in your own words)	REMEMBER the truth (Bible verse)
1. I will always be alone because I will never marry.	Marriage is not the only way to define relationship. God has promised to never leave me nor forsake me. Friends, family, and my church family are additional blessings in my life.	"I will never leave you nor forsake you." Josh. 1:5 "A cord of three strands is not quickly broken." Eccl. 4:12

RECOGNIZE	REPLACE	REMEMBER
2. I must always show joy for my friends getting married and having children. My own struggles have no place in those conversations.	Joy and suffering can coexist. There is a time and a place to safely and appropriately express the myriad of emotions we feel.	Eccl. 3:1-8 "In all this you greatly rejoice, though now for a little while you may have had to suffer grief in all kinds of trials." 1 Peter 1:6
3. I can't break up with this guy because then I will be alone.	God and others love me too much to see me in an unhealthy relationship.	"Perfect love drives out fear." 1 John 4:18
4. I have always dreamed of being a mom. When I find the right man, we will have children together, raise them in the Lord, and my dreams will have all come true!	If a woman is not complete in Christ, she will never find fulfillment in a marriage relationship or through children.	
5. God promises that everyone will get married eventually.	God does not promise marriage, but He does provide many promises about relationships.	

RECOGNIZE	REPLACE	REMEMBER
6. Everyone else is getting engaged or is already married. There must be something wrong with me that no one loves me.		
7. As a divorced woman, I am damaged goods that no one will ever love.		
8. I am in a holding pattern until I get married.		
9.		

May you be blessed by this list of additional verses, provided by single and single-again women in response to the question: "Please share a Bible verse that has encouraged you as a single woman."

Genesis 8:22

Exodus 14:10-14

Joshua 1:9

Book of Ruth, esp. 2:12

Psalm 16:8; 18:2; 23; 25:5; 37:4; 68:6;

Psalm 84:11; 103:13-14; 139; 143:8

Proverbs 3:5-6; 16:3; 19:21

Song of Solomon 2:7. 3:5, 8:4

Isaiah 41:10, 13; 54; 61; 66:9

Jeremiah 29:11

Joel 2:28

Habakkuk 3:18

Mark 12:30

Luke 1:46-50

John 16:33	2 Cor. 2:15	2 Timothy 1:7
Romans 8:18, 28; 15:13	Philippians 4:13	1 Peter 4:1-2
	1 Thess. 4:11	
1 Cor. 7:7-8, 32-35; 10:3; 11:9	2 Thess. 3:5	

Select one of the above Bible verses and fill in the Lie/Truth Chart going the other direction. Start with the truth REMEMBERED through the Bible verse. Then, in the REPLACE column, write out that promise in your own words. As you are writing out those truths from Scripture and in your own words, you will likely RECOGNIZE a specific lie with which Satan attacks you. Write that lie in the first column

RECOGNIZE the lie (in your own words)	REPLACE the lie with truth (in your own words)	REMEMBER the truth (Bible verse)

It is my prayer that you are equipped with a tool to remember the truth for yourself, but also to support others with reminders of truth through Scripture. God's Word is powerful, active, and can cut through the lies in a way that nothing else can (Heb. 4:12).

In the throes of our feelings of loneliness, in the midst of a personal attack by Satan, we may not have the presence of mind to reach out to another sister in Christ for her support. The good news is that God has given us the Holy Spirit as a reminder of truth. *"But the Helper, the Holy Spirit, whom the Father will send in my name, he will teach you all things and bring to your remembrance all that I have said to you"* (John 14:26, ESV).

Even though she doesn't mention the Holy Spirit by name, we can see how He has walked with Kayla through part of her story, shared below:

> I am 22 years old, have never had any adult boyfriends (I had a bus boyfriend in 8th grade), never a first kiss, or any real relationships with a guy. I had a few crushes (That's a lie. I have had a LOT of crushes) growing up, but all my experiences were not great.
>
> My best friends growing up were males, and when puberty hit guys got weird, and that basically got rid of any male friends I had. I survived elementary and middle school, only to arrive in high school and be swarmed with weird, wild males who did drugs, drank, or were sketchy. My biggest problem has been my smile because I smile all day every day, and I smile at everyone which attracts some weird yet interesting suitors. Eventually, I became extremely depressed because I couldn't attract any males I was attracted to, so I turned to "singles events." This was how I started down a bad battle with depression that I had to face by myself; I was growing more and more hopeless, even to the point of wanting to end it all.
>
> The last singles' event I attended was about a year or two ago and was the worst one I have ever been to. The nicest way I can describe the women who were attending was ladies who were so alone that they had to whine about their loneliness and how they didn't have a man every 5 minutes. This event changed my outlook to "I cannot be them!" **So, I started focusing more on my relationship and love for God and only God.** I stopped going to singles events, and eventually, I have found certain contentment of being single and having freedom. The ladies in the church are very pushy sometimes, but they're harmless, and I have found myself not feeling like I want or need a man to survive.
>
> I do go through bouts of feeling like I need a partner, and a few times I have listened to the dark side of my mind telling me I'm not good enough or not feminine enough. In those dark moments, I have even contemplated having a relationship with a woman instead of a man, but thoughts just such as those and others don't last. **What holds my**

focus the most is reading God's Word and remembering that He has a plan for each of us, and if we don't let God lead, we will fail.

Thank you for your transparency, Kayla, and for allowing God to use your story and the reminders of truth from His Word to guide and encourage you!

Listen now to Erica's story and the lies and fears she struggled with earlier in life.

I have had a life full of blessings and friends. When I was younger, I was raised to expect to find a husband and to find my worth in honoring God, by being a wife and mother. That is not the path that God has chosen for me thus far. I feel that this has helped me to be a servant in ways that being married or being a mother never would have allowed. There are so many responsibilities as a mother/wife that time can get away from you. I do probably work more than most for a paycheck, because I am my sole provider, and that does get tough sometimes as well... However, I am always able and willing to help out and to coordinate events going on around me with my church family and community. Because of these opportunities, I have been adopted into more families than I know what to do with. Being single has moments where you question the why of missing out on companionship, but the joy that I have found in service to my God far exceeds the want of that desire. I do not have any biological children, but because of the work that God has allowed me to be a part of, I now have 10 that call me Aunt Erica and love to have sleepovers and Bible studies at my house. The best thing is, they want to invite all of their friends. I never feel alone.

I have learned that happiness is found through the contentment of being what God has called you to be during your present state, and to seek His will joyfully with the aroma of Christ.

I hear many of the truths from 1 Corinthians 7 in Erica's story and how God has guided her on her journey toward the contentment she has now found in Him.

Using either Kayla's or Erica's story, fill in the Lie/Truth Chart below for her. Feel free to add a second line with a lie you have recognized and a truth you need to replace it with. Don't forget to remember the truth through a specific scripture!

RECOGNIZE the lie (in your own words)	REPLACE the lie with truth (in your own words)	REMEMBER the truth (Bible verse)

A widowed sister in Texas shared, "Although days can be lonely, you never are because God's got your back and He is with me always, so you are able to have a closer relationship with God as this is who you talk with daily."

[16] And I will ask the Father, and he will give you another Helper, to be with you forever, [17] even the Spirit of truth, whom the world cannot receive, because it neither sees him nor knows him. You know him, for he dwells with you and will be in you. (John 14:16-17)

Kari A., a divorced mom is grateful for "a really nice necklace that I wear a lot. [My sister] got it for me that next birthday. It says 'Redeemed' and that's always a good reminder."

Whether the reminders of truth come from the Holy Spirit or another person, we feel supported when we are lovingly led into that truth. Truth facilitates a closer walk with God and with one another. As we will affirm in the next section, **the most supportive people are those who take the time to listen to the desires of our heart, then point us to the only One who can fulfill them.**

Let's support one another by offering a PEAR: Prayer, Encouragement, Activities, and Reminders of Truth. My dear single sister, you are loved. You are prayed for. And you are not alone.

Table Talk

I am grateful that God has provided Aarons and Hurs of support in my life (Ex. 17:11-12). They have offered a PEAR when I get discouraged that I don't have "the other half of my orange" (as my Hispanic abuelas would say).

As we take a moment to reflect on and continue the conversation about Supporting One Another, begin with a moment of thanksgiving for the Aarons and Hurs in your own life, and the opportunities you have had to lift others' arms in support in the midst of their battles.

Talk with God (Reflection Questions)

How have you experienced support from others? And what support have you been able to provide for others? Your stories may fit into the categories of PEAR: Prayer, Encouragement, Activities, Reminders of Truth, but it's okay if they don't! We are celebrating the many ways in which we can show support.

Do you have any other takeaways from this section?

Talk with an Iron Rose Sister

Is there a specific lie you are currently battling in which an Iron Rose Sister can offer you confidential support? We want to allow God to use each other to offer Reminders of Truth. Let's commit to memorizing each other's Bible verse.

RECOGNIZE the lie (in your own words)	REPLACE the lie with truth (in your own words)	REMEMBER the truth (Bible verse)

 Remember, the **Common Threads** (which come from all other Iron Rose Sister Ministries' Small Group Bible Studies[15]) are shared with at least one other person in order that we can serve as iron sharpening iron (Prov. 27:17), encouraging each other to be as beautiful as a rose, in spite of a few thorns.

 An area in which you want to grow or bloom

A thorn you'd like to remove (a lie you've recognized)

An area in which you'd like to dig deeper or need someone to hold you accountable (the truth you want to remember and why)

Table Talk with One Another (one-on-one or group discussion)

Tell me about a time when you saw the impact of prayer in your life. How can I specifically pray for you and support you through prayer?

---

[15] For more information about Iron Rose Sister Ministries, our small group Bible study materials, and other resources, including additional resources for facilitating this conversation with single women or church leaders, see Chapter 34, "About Iron Rose Sister Ministries," and visit our website, https://IronRoseSister.com/.

What kinds of things are of greatest encouragement to you? Is there something others have done in the past they thought was an encouragement, but that was actually discouraging? (No names, please!)

What is your reaction to the three statements mentioned in the Activities chapter? Do you feel defensive, affirmed, challenged, or reminded to think of others in these ways?

- Single women are not a project. We are people.
- Singleness is not a problem to be fixed.
- We are all vital members of the body. We need each other.

On an individual level (not corporate level), what is an activity we can help make happen and who are at least five single or single-again women we can invite to join us?

Which Bible verses offered the most impactful Reminders of Truth?

Walk the Talk

What are specific **Action Steps** you can take this week to support and encourage a single woman by offering a PEAR (Prayer, Encouragement, Activities, Reminders of Truth)? I encourage you to make note of one single action step for each PEAR.

Prayer

Encouragement

Activities

Reminders of Truth

Tips for Small Group Table Talk[16]

An excellent memory tool for this lesson is to serve sliced pears as a snack.

A blank Lie/Truth Chart is available to download and print on the Iron Rose Sister Ministries website and can be found along with other "Free Resources." (https://IronRoseSister.com/)

---

[16] Don't forget the additional tools shared in Section VII, Chapter 30, "Small Group Discussion Recommendations."

Section III

Identifying the Deepest Desires of our Heart

Delight yourself in the Lord, and he will give you the desires of your heart.
(Ps. 37:4, ESV)

What are the deepest desires of your heart? Many little girls would put a pillowcase on the top of their heads as a veil and march down the hallway, envisioning their Prince Charming waiting for them. Their princess dreams of a happily ever after were not the same dreams I shared. My dreams were of being a mom to lots and lots of kids.

The oldest of four girls, I "mothered" my sisters. I would nurse my baby dolls under my shirt, swaddle them in blankets, and think through name combinations that I would give my many future children. Early on, I decided it would be cool to share my middle name, Joy, with any daughters I had, which meant that any girls' names I selected had to sound good with "Joy."

In the sixth grade, I wrote a paper on international adoption... way before this was a more common practice as it is today. I volunteered in the nursery as a teenager, babysat, nannied two summers, always offered to hold others' babies, especially during church, and I became an expert at getting them to sleep and at changing diapers swiftly.

I have lost count of the times that people asked me when I was going to have one of my own. The Venezuelans, while I lived there as a missionary, were especially relentless in their encouragement when they saw me holding a baby. My favorite response was, "It's a process..." I would enumerate and elaborate on the steps in the process, starting with the need to find the right man to marry with whom to have said babies, and then, a minimum of nine months later, possibly have the first one.

Years later, after having seen many single women choose to adopt, I realized that I might have chosen that path earlier in life or at least presented another direction to the Venezuelans when I answered, "It's a process..."

As you may have surmised, neither with a husband nor through adoption have I had any children. Yet the desire to be a mom still remained.

"Delight yourself in the Lord and He will give you the desires of your heart," right?! Most definitely right, but those desires may not come to be realized in the original way one envisioned.

I remember vividly the first time I realized that I had taken part in several international adoptions. Looking around my living room at a college girls' Bible study one evening, there were women from Venezuela, Nicaragua, Ghana, West Africa, and various states around the U.S., each with their own cultural diversity. I was humbled and joyful at the realization, but Satan continued to attack and tried to convince me that the desires of my heart were unfulfilled.

Loneliness would overwhelm my emotions. Lies about being unlovable would bombard my thoughts. And I would begin to focus more on what I thought I lacked than the blessings for which I could be grateful.

God has been patient with me as He has revealed and transformed the fulfillment of my deepest desires. Allow me to share a specific instance of the transformation of my heart's desire to be a mom.[17]

---

[17] Your desires may not be the same as mine, but God meets us where we are to reveal and transform the deepest desires of our heart.

CHAPTER 9

When God Transforms
the Desires of our Heart

God sets the lonely in families... (Ps. 68:6a, NIV)

Some friends of mine had their second child, a baby girl, on a Monday evening in February. Noah James was excited to welcome his baby sister, while mom and dad shared in the inexpressible joy of having a healthy baby born into the world.

I woke up on Tuesday to her beautiful picture on Facebook and my heart filled with joy for them—not only a joy in the birth of a new child, but also the reminder of the transformation we can have in Christ when we surrender our lives to Him.

Tia and Charlie were active students at the LSU Christian Student Center where I served as Women's Campus Minister for six years. Theirs is a story of God's power and the Spirit working in their lives. If I were to tell you some of the stories from when we first met, you would not even recognize the children of God that they are today! To make a long story short, within the course of a year, Tia was baptized, they were married, and Charlie was baptized!

Tia continued to attend the weekly girls' Bible study in my home and when she became pregnant with their first child, she shared with us the size of the baby as it compared to a fruit or vegetable. The gender wasn't revealed, nor the name, until he was born: Noah James.

I was blessed with the honor of being the first one to take care of him so that mom and dad could go on a date. Noah James knew my voice, and I was always available to hold him any time we were at church together. However, before his first birthday, I moved away.

The timing of my departure was coupled with a profound grief at the realization that I would not be able to birth any children of my own.

Less than a year later, when I received the news that they were expecting again, I was thrilled for them and their growing Christian family. I was also profoundly sad, having triggered the grief of my unmet expectations to be a mom. Joy and sorrow volleyed for highest rank amongst my compounding feelings.

Then, the greatest source of joy came a few minutes after I hit "like" on the baby's newborn picture on Facebook that cold Tuesday morning. Along with another picture of the baby, Tia texted me with the following statement, which I humbly share as a reminder of God's promise of redemption and with much hope for the transformation of the desires of your heart.

"Meet Abigail Joy. Named after the woman who gave me a thirst for the Living Water. Love you."

I almost couldn't finish reading the text as my eyes filled with grateful tears and inexpressible joy. It was a testimony to God's transformation of the deepest desires of my heart—not children I birthed in the traditional sense or daughters with whom I could share my middle name, Joy. Rather, a reminder of spiritual children having children of their own and the honor of calling them spiritual grandchildren. I knew in that moment that this baby girl, Abigail Joy, would be a source of joy and truth in my life and in the lives of many others.

I am honored to have been a small part of this family's journey and am thrilled to see them pass on a hunger and thirst for God and godly living to their now four children. Their one single reason is love—for God and for their children. And my single reason is no different.

Isaiah 54:1-8 reminds us,

> *"Sing, O barren one, who did not bear;*
> *break forth into singing and cry aloud, you who have not been in labor!*
> *For the children of the desolate one will be more*
> *than the children of her who is married," says the Lord.*
> *2 "Enlarge the place of your tent,*
> *and let the curtains of your habitations be stretched out;*
> *do not hold back; lengthen your cords and strengthen your stakes.*
> *3 For you will spread abroad to the right and to the left,*
> *and your offspring will possess the nations*
> *and will people the desolate cities.*
>
> *4 "Fear not, for you will not be ashamed;*
> *be not confounded, for you will not be disgraced;*
> *for you will forget the shame of your youth,*
> *and the reproach of your widowhood you will remember no more.*
> *5 For your Maker is your husband, the Lord of hosts is his name;*
> *and the Holy One of Israel is your Redeemer,*
> *the God of the whole earth he is called.*
> *6 For the Lord has called you like a wife deserted and grieved in spirit,*
> *like a wife of youth when she is cast off, says your God.*
> *7 For a brief moment I deserted you,*
> *but with great compassion I will gather you.*
> *8 In overflowing anger for a moment I hid my face from you,*
> *but with everlasting love I will have compassion on you,"*
> *says the Lord, your Redeemer.* (ESV)

As single or single-again women, what specific promise in these verses from Isaiah holds special meaning for you? [If you are married, with or without children, how might you read this passage differently through the eyes of a single or single-again sister? [18]]

Isaiah 54 acknowledges frustrations, fears, grief, and feelings of abandonment or loneliness that many single and single-again women face. When the feelings of desertion are perceived to be never-ending, may we contrast that brief moment (Is. 54:7) with the Lord's everlasting love (Is. 54:8).

God's eternal love for you is His one single reason. His thoughts are not our thoughts, and His ways are not our ways (Is. 55:8-9), but everything that happens truly can be used to bring about good (Jer. 29:11; Rom. 8:28). **His love and His sovereignty invite us to trust when the desires of our heart and the emotions of our day overshadow the hope of His redemption in any and every situation.**

Name three top things you want in life—some of the deepest desires of your heart.

Now, look back at your list of desires. What is at the root of them? Is it relationship? Or purpose? Put an R (relationship) or a P (purpose) next to each of them. It may be a combination of the two.

Through my own life, an analysis of expressed desires from others, and in-depth study of God's Word, I have come to believe that **at the root of all desires are two deepest desires: relationship and purpose.** These are timeless longings that God has placed in us to draw us back

---

[18] There are some who have never seen this or other biblical passages through the lens of single women. Give yourself the grace to reread it. Pray that God opens your eyes of understanding to include the feelings a single sister might face when she reads this or other passages of the Bible.

to Him. Sometimes they are combined or are presented in tandem, as we see through the undertones of Isaiah 54.

An understanding of the cultural context of those desires can inform how they play out for women. For example, the culture in Bible times dictated that in order for a woman to have honor, status, a voice in the conversation, or a seat at the table, she had to have borne male offspring. Her primary source of honor and her purpose in society was to bear children. Jesus recognized this when He redeemed the widow of Nain from the deep agony of her son's death, raising him from the dead (Luke 7:11-15).

Jesus rose above the cultural norm for these desires in the lives of single women. He redeemed their relationships and their purpose. I delight in seeing the attention Jesus gave to widows (Mark 12:41-44; Luke 7:11-15), a possible former prostitute (Mary Magdalene), divorcees (John 4, the Samaritan woman—or yes, she could've been a five-time widow), single mothers (Syrophoenecian in Mark 7), and single women (Mary and Martha).

God truly sees and honors women from all walks of life, backgrounds, experiences, and reputations. I also marvel at Matthew's inclusion of the five women in Jesus' lineage (Matt. 1). Tamar, Rahab, Ruth, Bathsheba, and Mary—which do you identify with from her colorful past or the ways in which her peers might have criticized her?[19]

Through the transformation of the desires of her heart, God redeemed each woman's story, inviting her to be a part of the lineage of Christ. They are models of what it means to be true believers, especially when they continued to trust God as their original life plans

---

[19] If you don't know the stories of these fantastic women, I invite you to get to know them! **Tamar** in Genesis 38. **Rahab** in Joshua 2, 6:22-25. **Ruth** in the book of Ruth. **Bathsheba** in 2 Samuel 11-12; 1 Kings 1. **Mary** in Luke 1:26-56, 2:1-52.

or deepest desires didn't match up with God's greater plan for the answers to those desires. As followers of Christ, God calls us to trust Him with our relationships and our purpose. **We, as with the women in Jesus' genealogy, may not see the greater purpose God has for our lives and our relationships until much later down the road.**

In His teaching about what it means to truly be His disciple in John 15, Jesus reminds us that bearing fruit or making new disciples is the blessing and responsibility of all disciples (John 15:8). Matthew 28:18-20 echoes the same command.

¹⁸ And Jesus came and said to them, "All authority in heaven and on earth has been given to me. ¹⁹ Go therefore and make disciples of all nations, baptizing them in the name of the Father and of the Son and of the Holy Spirit, ²⁰ teaching them to observe all that I have commanded you. And behold, I am with you always, to the end of the age." (ESV)

The promise that Jesus will be with us "always, to the end of the age," is an affirmation of relationship and the fullness of a fulfilled purpose. **There is no disciple-making without relationship—with God and with others.** The Great Commission (Matt. 28:18-20) is the two deepest desires of our heart all rolled into one: deep relationship and meaningful purpose.

Returning to John 15:1-17, we see the language with which Christ describes the nature of the relationship with Him and with others— our one single reason.

In the quoted text from John 15, please underline all the references to Jesus, the Son. Double-underline any references to God, the Father. Put a heart around any form of the word "love." Circle any references to us (often referred to as "you" in the text). I started it for you.

"I am the true vine, and my Father is the vinedresser. ² Every branch in me that does not bear fruit he takes away, and every branch that does bear fruit he prunes, that it may bear more fruit. ³ Already you are clean because of the

word that I have spoken to you. *4*Abide in me, and I in you. As the branch cannot bear fruit by itself, unless it abides in the vine, neither can you, unless you abide in me. *5*I am the vine; you are the branches. Whoever abides in me and I in him, he it is that bears much fruit, for apart from me you can do nothing. *6*If anyone does not abide in me he is thrown away like a branch and withers; and the branches are gathered, thrown into the fire, and burned. *7*If you abide in me, and my words abide in you, ask whatever you wish, and it will be done for you. *8*By this my Father is glorified, that you bear much fruit and so prove to be my disciples. *9*As the Father has loved me, so have I loved you. Abide in my love. *10*If you keep my commandments, you will abide in my love, just as I have kept my Father's commandments and abide in his love. *11*These things I have spoken to you, that my joy may be in you, and that your joy may be full.

12"This is my commandment, that you love one another as I have loved you. *13*Greater love has no one than this, that someone lay down his life for his friends. *14*You are my friends if you do what I command you. *15*No longer do I call you servants, for the servant does not know what his master is doing; but I have called you friends, for all that I have heard from my Father I have made known to you. *16*You did not choose me, but I chose you and appointed you that you should go and bear fruit and that your fruit should abide, so that whatever you ask the Father in my name, he may give it to you. *17*These things I command you, so that you will love one another." (ESV)

What other words or imagery are used for relationship? Don't forget to mention who is in that relationship description.

Describe or illustrate what you now understand to be facets of our purpose (from John 15).

Our Creator designed us to be in relationship with Him and for that to be our singular purpose. When sin entered in, the deceiver distorted how those desires were to be fulfilled. As our Redeemer, when we walk with God every step of the way, He can use every part of our story in the fulfillment of purpose and blessing in relationships. He draws us back into relationship with Him and uses us as His instruments to invite others into relationship with Him—our ultimate purpose.

Whether in the context of relationship or purpose, we have to be open enough to let God transform our limited definition of our desires. **If I hold too tightly to the details of my dreams, I cheapen the lavish ways in which God longs to fulfill them.** As affirmed by their responses to the survey questions, in interviews, and in other conversations, other single and single-again women agree that trusting God for the fulfillment of our desires allows Him to transform and answer our prayers in ways that are beyond what we can ask or imagine. We will explore each of those two desires more specifically in the following two chapters.

CHAPTER 10

The Desire for Deep Relationship

'And you shall love the Lord your God with all your heart and with all your soul and with all your mind and with all your strength.' The second is this: 'You shall love your neighbor as yourself.' There is no other commandment greater than these. (Mark 12:30-31, ESV)

Our identity is not defined by a marriage relationship, but rather our relationship with God and our relationships with one another. Of the more than eighty "one another" statements in the New Testament, less than 15% refer directly to a marriage relationship. All others are applicable to any and all of the relationships in our lives. The description of love in 1 Corinthians 13, while a beautiful text to share during the wedding ceremony and marriage vows, is equally reflective of the relationship goals with Christian brothers and sisters, coworkers, and even enemies.

When God stated that it is not good for man to be alone (Gen. 2), the priority was on relationship. Yes, procreation was important. Yes, God designed Eve to be a helpmeet and lifelong partner for Adam. However, when God first saw that it was good, it was in the context of each of them being created in His image. *"Male and female He created them"* (Gen. 1:27). In the previous verse, we see God refer to Himself in the plural, *"Let us make man in our image, in our likeness"* (Gen. 1:26, NIV). The plural personal pronoun is indicative of the relational nature of God Himself—Father, Son, and Spirit. God is One, the One true God, but even He demonstrates the inherent relational nature in whose image we were created.

When single and single-again women answered the question, "What is the greatest blessing as a single Christian woman?", the most common answer was freedom or independence. The second most-mentioned blessing was her relationship with God. This corresponds with the most common answer to the question regarding the greatest challenge as a single Christian woman: loneliness, lack of relationship, or a longing to belong.

When I interviewed Bethany, the youngest adult daughter of a divorced single mom, she delighted in naming the people from church and from the neighborhood that mowed her mom's yard, provided food, and cleaned the house, especially while her mom, Lis, was in the hospital battling cancer. Bethany continued,

> Things like that... just how much love there is for each other. And all of it comes from God's love. And that was another thing, when my mom got her diagnosis. I told her, "You are the strongest person I know." You know, from seeing all the things that had happened in the past with her marriage and with our family. And she said, "Well, my strength comes from God. And yours does, too." And I was like, "I wish I could say that, but I can't. I'm not there. I know it should, but I haven't reached that point where I can confidently say that." And she said, "Well, I probably would have said the same thing at 23 years old."
>
> My relationship with God in general is something I'm still working on. I'm not great at making myself study and pray... I think it just reminds me to love others the way that God loves them and to just love them unconditionally no matter what. And to really see their heart, not just

surface level things. Those friendships and relationships show God to me.

Our relationship with God informs our relationships with one another. And conversely, as Bethany expressed, our relationships with others influence our relationship with God. Considering these and other filters we use to view our relationships, I am reminded, specifically, of how many of us allow relationships with men to cast a far-reaching shadow on our relationship with God. At different stages in our lives, we may or may not believe that our relationship with God can be one of a loving, Heavenly Father who showers unconditional love on His precious daughters.

When a woman is not in a healthy marital or dating relationship, she more easily doubts God's love for her and whether she is able to be loved by others. Ladies, it is my prayer that we will find confidence and completeness in God's love. Only He can complete us.

Tears streaming down the face of many young women, their questions of "Why?" come out in a whimper. "What's wrong with me?" "Why does no one love me?" The frustrated cries of loneliness rooted in doubts echo in my mind from countless conversations with single women. Single-again women, especially those separated or divorced, wrestled with similar questions, including additional layers of rejection, abandonment, and disillusionment.

Cultural or societal identity is dependent on our relationships, especially marital relations. "Oh, you're divorced." "No, I'm single." "Yes, I'm here by myself."

For years, I cringed when asked the question if I was married. I felt like my answer, "No," meant that I had something to be ashamed of. And when the follow up question about whether I was dating someone required another negative response, **my negations felt like affirmations that something was wrong with me**. The survey responses were filled with similar sentiments, coupled with other statements riddled with doubts and uncertainties, not exclusively among the younger respondents.

Over time, God has comforted me. He has led me to the affirmations in His Word. He has provided others who have supported me and encouraged me with reminders of truth. Now, I have come to look forward to answering the question about whether or not I am married. My response? "Yes, I am—to Christ and His church. He's the best husband ever!"

Isaiah 54 and 2 Corinthians 11:2 affirm that our Maker is our husband and that we are betrothed to one husband, Christ. **The intimate language used for our relationship with God, not to mention the language in Song of Solomon, reflects the depth of love, level of intimacy, and complete fulfillment that only a relationship with God can provide.**

Tammie was filled with questions of doubt about her self-worth and her desire to be loved by a man. Listen to part of her story after her second divorce.

Coming out of this divorce, there are things I feel rejuvenated about, but there are still a lot of questions. I prayed and prayed and prayed and God brings it to *them*, but not to me. That is part of what I struggle with.

"God, you know that I want to know what it means to be truly loved. I have had two husbands who didn't know how to love."

There has been a lot of questioning. [After my first divorce], I was more in pain, so it was an avoiding God because I was in pain, and I didn't know God could heal me. This time I know God can heal me, there's just a lot of, "Okay God, I get that it happens for a reason, but I don't understand."

There is that longing to be loved by a man the way I should be. There is that longing because I want to know what that feels like. I don't think there's anything wrong with a woman who wants to know what that feels like. Then I think of the ones who have never been married... it hurts me. But I want those women to know what it feels like too.

I run into people that are like, "I've got God. I've got Jesus. I'm good." I've got God and I've got Jesus too, but I want a little bit more. There are some women who can handle that. I am not one of those. It will be a struggle, but I have to sit back and... it's tough.

It is tough! As Tammie shared openly about her struggles, I know that many can relate. You are not alone. Whether a woman has never been married or has been married twice, like Tammie, we all have questions, doubts, and desires to be deeply loved. We are motivated by that one single reason of love, but we cannot allow our desire for "love" in a human relationship to supersede our number one priority of a loving relationship with God.

God, who is love, is the only one who can truly, deeply, completely, and unconditionally love. No matter whether you are currently or ever were married, God must be the number one relationship in our lives (Luke 14:25-33; Matt. 6:33).

In the first section, I alluded to the fact that many perceive that churches idolize marriage. While I still believe that to be true, I want to challenge us, single ladies, on that same point. Anyone who focuses on a spouse who can complete them is idolizing that spouse and is also idolizing marriage—putting a person or a thing in the place of God.

Singleness provides us with the opportunity to intentionally and completely rely on God. This need becomes more acute when a single woman is seeking someone with whom to have meaningful conversation or a single-again woman is missing the person who provided physical companionship.

It is difficult sometimes. God is good and He loves me, but He's not holding my hand at night while we watch a movie or go out to eat. The simple things in life are the ones I miss the most.

A single sister explained that the greatest challenge is, "trying to piece together a stable support system. People move, become absorbed in their own families and children. I have to work very hard to create a makeshift family and it changes around much more often than I would like."

As with these two surveyed women, we all share a longing to love and to be loved. Among all those surveyed, **there were more expressions of a desire for a family than for a husband**—whether dreams of being a mother or being able to experience healthy family-style loving relationships within the church. One of the common challenges expressed by many is when it appears that some people's prayers for any of those types of relationships are being answered when others' prayers are not.

Let me rewind a moment to an earlier segment of Tammie's story:

I was 22 and what I call "young, dumb, and stupid." I met, got engaged, and got married within a month to a man who was not anything of what... well, I didn't listen to anybody. It's what I tell people, "He was my black knight on a white horse and all I saw was the white horse." ... He wouldn't let me go to church. His dad was a Pentecostal preacher. That's the other thing. He was Pentecostal. I was Church of Christ. And we got married by a Baptist preacher. We laughed at that. There was a lot of abuse, from physical to spiritual. When he kicked me out, it was losing the kids (he had four children from a previous marriage) that was hard. We were already talking about how I was going to adopt the kids. I had just turned 24 in August, and we got divorced in October.

It took me five years of grieving the kids. In that five years, it was really tough. I had been a mom. I loved being a mom, but there was all the trauma and all the things that changed me. Because of the abuse, there was a lot of low self-esteem...

It was fourteen years between when I divorced and when I married my second husband. I always wanted children. Thought I would be married by then and have children.

Going through all of [the online dating] made me question God, "Why haven't I found someone else?" There are other women who have gone through divorces, and they meet someone and they find a good guy...

"What am I...? Why?" I went through a long process with God. Sometimes I was talking to Him, sometimes I wasn't. It was a very struggling time because it hurt. "God, you know I want to be married. God, you know that's what I want." Fast forward to now. **I *still* have that question: How come some people's prayer gets answered and other people's don't, when that is their deepest desire?**

Five years ago, I started going to Celebrate Recovery®[20]. That really started to change my internal dialogue and really helped me because I had abandonment, I had the divorce, I had trauma, I had abuse. I had all that. So, to deal with all of that, it helped, and it helped my relationship with Jesus.

Tammie's deepest desire was to be a wife and mom. She cried out to God to answer that prayer. And as of this moment, He has not answered her prayer in the way she has asked.

What encouragement would you offer Tammie or what encouragement do you think she would want to offer you?

Intimacy of Relationship

Tammie wanted others to be encouraged by her story and to learn from some of her mistakes. She is still discovering who God has called her to be and what relationships in her life will help draw her closer to God or which ones will push her away from Him. That is an excellent filter: **Will this relationship draw me closer to God or distract me from fully loving Him?**

Intimacy is for the purpose of holiness, not happiness. Therefore, if you are seeking happiness in marriage or in any friendship, you are looking for the wrong kind of relationship. The intentionality with which we enter into any relationship should be an outpouring or a

---

[20] Celebrate Recovery® is a Christ-centered 12 step program. https://www.celebraterecovery.com/

byproduct of our primary relationship with God. **The body of Christ and the family of Christ are the storehouses of deep relationship.** But if we don't start with the foundation of a solid relationship with God, we won't have a base from which to define or redefine all other relationships.

An intentionality of intimacy should always seek God first. That priority should then inform all other relationships through God's definition of how they should be lived out. And if we or someone we know is not living out God's definition of relationships, we should, through our one single reason, be able to hold each other accountable to that type of holy living. As Tyson and Grizzle state in *A Creative Minority*, "Having a covenant community means we choose accountable unity over loose networks."[21] Nominal Christians cannot fulfill each other's longings for depth of relationship. We must go deeper than Sunday morning encounters.

Intimacy facilitates accountability. One of my favorite relational descriptions is that we live as iron sharpening iron (Prov. 27:17). I have had the blessing of a diverse group of women in my life who have served as iron sharpening iron, accountability partners, or Iron Rose Sisters, as I call them. They have encouraged me to be as beautiful as a rose, in spite of a few thorns. They have spoken the truth in love (Eph. 4:15) when a thorn is a sin that needs to be removed. And when that thorn is one like Paul describes in 2 Corinthians, they remind me that God's *"grace is sufficient for [me], for [His] power is made perfect in weakness"* (2 Cor. 12:9, ESV).

Relational weaknesses can come from past hurts, intimacy, and trust issues. Poor examples of marriage and post-divorce culture contribute to a desire for avoidance. Thankfully, whether we are living out the consequences of others' decisions or our own sin, God's forgiveness is great, and His power of redemption is infinite. He is not

---

[21] Jon Tyson and Heather Grizzle. *A Creative Minority: Influencing Culture Through Redemptive Participation.* (Coppell, TX: self-published. 2016), 20.

punishing you for your past (another lie of Satan). Rather, His love redefines us and the blood of His Son clothes us with gleaming white robes (Rev. 7:9-14).

Sisters, take a deep breath in the hope of that statement. **God's love is what defines you, not any relationship you have or have not had.**

Romantic Love

Some advice from kids on love and romance: "I'm not rushing into love. Fourth grade is hard enough" (Regina, age ten). When asked, "What are some ways to make someone fall in love with you?" Alonzo, age nine answered, "Don't do things like have smelly, green sneakers. You might get attention, but attention ain't the same thing as love."[22]

If only love and relationships were that easy!

True love and deep relationships are not easy, but with humility and faith like a child (Matt. 18:3), God can guide them and transform the desires of our heart through them. His mercies are new every morning (Lam. 3:22-23).

God's definition of love (agape) is our "one single reason," but romantic love (eros) can be one of the most deceptive types of love. C.S. Lewis cautions,

> Every human love, at its height, has a tendency to claim for itself a divine authority. Its voice tends to sound as if it were the will of God Himself. It tells us not to count the cost, it demands of us a total commitment, it attempts to override all other claims and insinuates that any action which is sincerely done "for love's sake" is thereby lawful and even meritorious.[23]

---

[22] Edward K. Rowell and *Leadership*, editors. *1001 Quotes, Illustrations, and Humorous Stories for Preachers, Teachers, and Writers.* (Grand Rapids, Michigan: Baker Books. 2008), 344.

[23] C.S. Lewis. *The Four Loves.* (New York: Harcourt Brave. 1960), 7.

It is amazing to me how many times I have heard women justify their decisions in unhealthy relationships, even stating that God placed that person in her life. Ladies, your soulmate is never another woman's husband. And even if you are not entering into sexual intimacy with a married man, relational intimacy can be equally dangerous and potentially sinful with the wrong person, be that a man or a woman. What God has designed to be beautiful and magnificent, can be distorted by Satan.

Not everything done "for love's sake" is truly done out of the selfless love that God Himself embodied when He sacrificially sent His Son to become the perfect sacrifice. Living out love, for Jesus, meant that His relationship with God was at the center of everything. He knew and trusted His Father, even to the point of death.

The ways in which Jesus lived out love as a single man are our standards for intimate relationships with God and with one another.

Following Jesus' example, when we place God first and live out our love for Him, we allow Him to inform every other relationship. We put ourselves in the hands of the One who parted the Red Sea, raised Lazarus from the dead, sacrificed His Son... and is capable of doing beyond what we can ask or imagine. How can we not trust His plan, His design, and His purpose in relationships?

With 20/20 hindsight on more than one occasion, I have seen God give me a deeper desire for relationship and purpose in Him by not giving me what I specifically prayed for. **God has honored the deepest desires of my heart instead of being limited by my own definitions or by society's messages—both cheap versions of how those relationship desires might be incompletely fulfilled.**

But not everyone has understood or respected my imperfect journey. When I was younger, the compromises were presented in tempting ways and the ridicule was about not adopting a certain practice for myself. Same sex couples making out in the hallways of my high school was an everyday occurrence. Stretching relational boundaries with a guy to get him or keep him was common practice. As my years of singleness have prolonged, the pressure has shifted to attempts to get me to entertain and approve of relational practices outside of God's design (Rom. 1:26-32).

The expectations that culture and marketing ads project onto single women can be overwhelming. Temptations to compromise God's design for relationships and to fall into sinful substitutes are rampant. And if we do not engage in conversations that first seat God at the head of the table, celebrating God's ultimate plan for intimate relationships, especially those for single women, it is easy to fall into the trap of sin.

It is also easy to assume that others are participating in these errant practices. More than one family member has asked whispered questions about whether I was attracted to women. Two respondents to the survey specifically mentioned that one of their greatest challenges as a single woman was "people thinking you're gay."

Entire books have been dedicated to the conversation about LGBTQ+ relationships. That is not this book, but the conversations facilitated through this book will likely touch on that topic. This is one of the other marginalized groups to which I have referred. God has a lot to say on this topic and I recommend, as with all of these conversations, that we first invite God to His seat at the head of the table—the same table where we want everyone to have a place from which to join in the conversation.

Conversations about gender identity, sexual attraction, natural and unnatural relations are best had through the filter of our one single reason (agape love). **If love for God and love for the person with whom we are conversing are not our primary reason to engage in the conversation, we should not presume to be able to be a respected voice in that discussion.**

Am I looking to my own interests or to the interests of others? Am I being patient and kind? Am I loving through humility or with arrogant boasting?

As my mom poignantly summarized in her longing to lovingly express biblical truths to a young single woman who didn't want to hear them, "She may not accept my faith. Her situation, in her own words, feels hopeless. But showing her God's love is the way in which I can keep the conversation open." Amen!

Let's continue to live out love in our relationships with God and with one another. What would you like to add to this conversation about our desire for deep relationship? What else does God say about our relationships?

CHAPTER 11

The Desire for Meaningful Purpose

A three-year-old girl listened intently to the children's sermon. The minister explained that God wants everyone to get along

*and love each other. "God wants us all to be one," he said.
To which the girl replied, "But I don't want to be one. I want to be four!"*[24]

"**I** want to serve God!" "How can I find God's purpose for my life?" "I want to be part of something bigger... to make a difference in people's lives."

High school and college students readily express their desire for meaningful purpose as they debate career choices, pray fervently to be led by God down the right path, and seek to make the right decisions about where to live, what relationships to pursue, etc.

Those same questions and longings do not change over time. **The majority of single women, through the surveys and interviews, overwhelmingly echoed the desire to serve God and others.** Their mutual desire for purpose and service was interchangeable in the language. I applaud these women for seeing that God's definition of purpose is others-focused and is a success that is not as the world might define it (Matt. 5:1-12).

In seeking God's design for our lives through relationship and through purpose, Christ's example of seeking God's will over our own is pivotal (Matt. 26:36-44). **God does not call everyone to literally die on a cross, but He does call us to die to ourselves daily by taking up our cross and following Him (Matt. 16:24; Luke 9:23).** Love is the one single reason that makes any sacrifice worthwhile. And many times, living out a meaningful purpose requires sacrifice.

"As a single woman, it is easy to find ways to serve within my local congregation." Sixty-seven percent of women surveyed agreed or

---

[24] Marilyn McCoy. Edward K. Rowell and *Leadership*, editors. *1001 Quotes, Illustrations, and Humorous Stories for Preachers, Teachers, and Writers.* (Grand Rapids, Michigan: Baker Books. 2008), 310.

strongly agreed with this statement. Age was not a factor that contributed to the validity of this statement for the participants.

For example, a single woman, never married, in her 50's offered,

I have taught Bible classes from Cradle Roll through Jr. High. I have led singing at Ladies' Days. I have organized Parents' Nights Out. I have served on committees and in the nursery. I spent several years going back and forth between happily single and wondering what was wrong with me, that no man loved me. Now I am content; if God brings someone into my life, I am open to that, but not actively looking or feeling inadequate.

Sometimes the opportunities to serve are found outside the walls of the church building.

I work full-time in a ministry-related job. Because I don't have a husband, kids, or other obligations at home, I'm able to throw everything into serving the kids and families at work. I usually work 80-100+ hours a week, and it allows me to meet the needs of kids and their families who have experienced exceptionally high levels of exposure to potentially traumatic events, and meet them where they're at with what they need. I simply couldn't do it without being single. "The woman who is unmarried, and the virgin, is concerned about the things of the Lord..."

In her interview, Susan affirmed the importance of modeling single life for others, especially those younger than her.

I recognize that I am given opportunities to model life for young women who may have never seen or don't have an example or a model to follow, who may end up living a very similar life. That's definitely an awareness that I have, and that also impacts how I try to live my life, the choices that I make, because I'm aware that I'm in an environment where people are watching what I'm doing... I don't wish this life for every woman. It's not for every woman. But I recognize more and more that young women are making a choice to live a life that's more similar to what I do than to what their mothers have done.

And Kristy, a single mom who was married for 22 years, now serves by helping the children in her neighborhood.

I have been able to concentrate more on God since my divorce. When I was married, my concentration seemed to always be on my husband. I have served by helping other children in the neighborhood who were from divorced families. Sometimes they might need a ride somewhere like the local recreation center or some of them just needed someone to talk to because of problems at home and others just like having a place to come at times to hang out with my son and eat a snack. I would like to be able to make a difference somewhere in life for someone, but I am not sure where that is right now. I just take it one day at a time and try to help whoever comes in my path and do what I can as a single mom/woman.

I think we can all agree that Kristy is making a difference in the lives of everyone she encounters. Susan is modeling Christian living for young single women. Each of these single women have found contentment in God and are striving to live out love through meaningful purpose, in service to others. Thank you, ladies! **You are modern day missionaries in the unique places God has called each of you to serve. We celebrate you and your stories.** May God be praised for how He is accomplishing His will through your lives to touch the lives of others.

For some, the opportunities to fulfill a purpose or meet a need would be easier if there were someone else with whom they could serve. As Tonda, a divorced mother and grandmother, expressed, "I know I can always teach children's Bible classes or a ladies' class, but that's not where my gifts and talents are. I haven't served much because I don't feel comfortable doing it alone." Meaningful purpose in service to God and to others may present itself as an opportunity to partner with someone else, serving together. We are not alone, ladies, and we are not called to go it alone.

What has meaningful purpose or service looked like in your life? How can you walk with someone else to encourage them to serve in an area you are both passionate about?

Single Women Missionaries

Thankfully, in our history, there are a number of single women missionaries, pivotal and instrumental in the spread of the gospel. I have had the honor and privilege of personally knowing hundreds of those single and single-again women, serving across the globe and across the street. It is my prayer that we can celebrate more of these modern and pioneering stories as an inspiration to other women longing to answer that call.

Dr. Shawn Daggett, professor of missions at Harding University, has researched these ground-breaking missionaries and chronicled much of the history of missions within the churches of Christ. When asked to share his comments on the matter, he made the following four observations:

1. In the history of missions of the churches of Christ, if you count both married and single women, the women have outnumbered men almost 2 to 1.

2. Although our missionary women have done medical work, opened and taught in schools, worked as and along with Bible women, offered hospitality, and served alongside their husbands... they have also planted churches, trained preachers, and continued the work of male missionaries when husbands were ill, died, or the male worker in the region left the country.

3. Generally speaking, women missionaries have presented a less threatening presence in many areas of the world where men would not be permitted to enter.

4. Many single women missionaries of the past believed or worked among churches that believed that men should be the leaders and preachers of the church. They therefore were able to train national workers and create a vacuum of leadership into which these local men would serve without competing with Western male missionaries who needed to validate their support and presence on the field through continuing their strong leadership.

What a blessing that this is a part of our history, ladies! I think that many of these stories, like Sarah Andrews' in the Introduction, are not celebrated or shared enough. Personally, I didn't know much of that history when I first felt called onto the mission field. God had to strip away every facet of the preconceptions and stereotypes I had come to believe limited my calling. Married? Nope. Going to a foreign country? Not initially. Working with a North American team? Nope.

What I had perceived to be the ideal was a North American team filled with exclusively married individuals who homeschooled their children in a foreign country. Not coincidentally, I have a number of friends that did serve God for many years across the world following a similar pattern. However, any stereotypes or assumptions cheapen the reality of all God did in and through those families through their service. When talking with them, I am always intentional about speaking with and about the woman as a missionary herself, not as a missionary's wife. Single or married, in a team or not, each of these women are living out love in the context God has called them.

In contrast to the models I had previously observed, when I moved to Venezuela as a single missionary, I worked with all Venezuelans. I had realized that it was important for me, personally, to emphasize my role as one of support, encouragement, and equipping rather than that of someone who might inadvertently create a North American church model or a dependence on foreign missionaries. I think it was also God's way of keeping me humble while calling me to rise to a challenge through which I grew tremendously in my dependence on Him.

"You Would Make a Good Missionary's Wife"

This was not my first visit to the city, nor my first evangelistic campaign in Latin America. In this particular location, we had built relationships with many of the local businesses and were offered reduced rates for housing, rented vehicles, etc. Knowing how things worked, when we first arrived, I strived to ensure that I would be one of the ones with the keys to drive the automatic Jeeps, leaving the standards to those who had more experience driving them. However, the automatics broke down with greater frequency and were often the first keys to be relinquished by the original drivers in order for others to make visits and conduct Bible studies.

One morning, the only Jeeps left available were the standards. Undeterred, my desire to conduct the Bible study won over my fear of driving a standard. I relied on my pioneering spirit, extensive powers of observation, and the intellectual know-how for driving a standard. A brave sister jumped in the Jeep with me, and we were off!

Yes, of course, there were many bumps along the way, including minor whiplash and stutter starts. It took longer to get there than it would've taken someone with more experience, but we finally arrived and studied the Bible with the lady who was waiting for us!

Later that week, with only standards left to drive (all the automatics were back in the shop), I accepted the challenge of practicing every time I could. However, one night, our group was running late for the evening campaign, and it was best for a more experienced driver to get us there more quickly and efficiently.

Halfway to the church building, the car died. In the attempts to get it going again, it started rolling back on the road into a large pile of sand and dirt. Determined to get to the church building, we needed a plan.

We quickly realized that it would take the four of us pushing with the driver ready to pop the clutch if we had any hope of getting out of the sandy dirt embankment. My toes curl at the memory of the grit that filled our shoes, attempting to get a good running start at pushing the Jeep.

However, the memory that sticks with me more painfully from that day was a comment by one of the men who was in the Jeep with us. When he saw my willingness to jump out, to get my feet and hands dirty, his reaction, meant as a compliment was, "You would make a good missionary's wife!"

As previously evidenced by my determined spirit and stubborn nature, his comment became a charge to rise to the challenge of being the best missionary I could be—not a missionary's wife—a missionary in my own right, whether I was married or not.

Around that same time, I was beginning to discover that the model of missionary couples and missionary teams did not fit the calling that God had given me. Woefully unaware of any other single women who had modeled that type of service, I had been constantly discouraged by others' insistence that it be a married couple who served.

Expectations and assumptions clouded my judgement and hindered my desire for purpose and service in the Kingdom. Thankfully, I found many who supported me and my desire to serve God as a single woman. Prayerfully, I have been able to serve as an example and inspiration to other single women who are seeking to serve God in ways they had not originally envisioned. Ladies, it is not an easy road, but it is a worthwhile one.

Each person's story is unique and the challenges that come with it can be daunting. In those difficult moments, remember the expression, **"But God..."**

I thought only married women could be missionaries, **but God** taught me that He provides opportunities for single women to serve, too. Another sister felt trapped by her life as a single mom with young kids at home, **but God** reminded her of the seeds being planted in her children and their friends' hearts when the van full of children sang

"Jesus Loves Me" at the top of their lungs on the way home from Vacation Bible School. A third sister, younger than the other two, feared that she was beyond forgiveness when others gave her critical stares, **but God** redeemed her story when she was invited to share it with young teenagers, encouraging them to avoid many of the mistakes she had made.

Sisters, I am humbled by the ways in which God steps into our stories and redirects them in ways only He can. **"But God!"** What Bible story comes to mind when I make that statement, "But God..."?

No matter your calling—ministry or missions, single or married, mother or aunt—allow God to use it to make you more holy, not more happy.

God uses *every* aspect of our stories to bring about His will, fulfill His purpose, and provide us with a path into deeper relationship with Him!

Please hear me when I say that I do not believe that God's will for your life or His purpose is a singular path that cannot be deviated from in the slightest without monumental repercussions. To live in that type of fear of a misstep is debilitating and even paralyzing. Our God is bigger than that.

God has given us free will. And He is bigger than any circumstances. What some intend for ill, He can work out for good (Joseph and his brothers; Gen. 50:20). The entire book of Genesis has been my greatest teacher about God's grace and His ability to work through and in spite of our shortcomings and weaknesses. "But God...!"

The apostle John reminds us that it is about walking with God in the light and not pretending that we will never make a mistake. If and when I do stray from His purpose for my life—to walk in relationship with Him—He offers me a way back through His Son. Repentance is about turning back to Him and away from that errant path.

⁵This is the message we have heard from him and proclaim to you, that God is light, and in him is no darkness at all. ⁶If we say we have fellowship with him while we walk in darkness, we lie and do not practice the truth. ⁷But if we walk in the light, as he is in the light, we have fellowship with one another, and the blood of Jesus his Son cleanses us from all sin. ⁸If we say we have no sin, we deceive ourselves, and the truth is not in us. ⁹If we confess our sins, he is faithful and just to forgive us our sins and to cleanse us from all unrighteousness. ¹⁰If we say we have not sinned, we make him a liar, and his word is not in us. (1 John 1:5-10, ESV)

The invitation in 1 John is a reminder of God's one single reason—His love and His desire to be in relationship with us. In turn, we, out of love for Him and love for others, have the opportunity to be a light to others, pointing them to the true source of light (Matt. 5:14-16). It is our truest calling and our greatest purpose.

Ladies, if you feel that you "missed the boat" of your purpose, please know that it is never too late. **No opportunity for service is too small.** And we, as single and single-again women, have a wealth of experience, passion, and ability to serve the Lord and His church.

Singleness is a gift through which we can allow God to use us as intentional Kingdom workers. "Opportunities" was the most frequently used word in the surveys when the women were asked about the most positive aspects of being single.

We cannot take advantage of every opportunity, but if we ask for wisdom, God promises to provide it (James 1:5), and He will guide us regarding which opportunities to say yes to and which ones may be a better fit for others to serve. As singles, assumptions about our level of independence, amount of availability, or abundance of time may be traps to avoid, but it is true that the decisions about our availability primarily lie within our control. We will continue the conversation about these and other kinds of assumptions in Section IV, Chapter 15.

Finally, what we pray for is only the tip of the iceberg—the part we think we see when God is working. However, God knows and sees the deeper desires at the root of our longing (e.g., to serve in a certain way). God can fully encompass the entire iceberg with His answers in His timing, Keep praying and bringing it to God... **He will honor the deepest desires of your heart for purpose and will answer in ways that are beyond what you ask or imagine.**

In the meantime, what is an opportunity to serve you can take advantage of and fulfill your purpose through? Or maybe there is a way in which God has already led you to live out love that we can celebrate with you?

CHAPTER 12

A Longing for Physical Affection

The desire for physical affection is a natural one. According to Gary Chapman's book, *The Five Love Languages*, physical touch, even for a married couple, is not to be exclusively expressed through the sexual act.

During quarantine under the ravages of COVID-19, many individuals, not just singles, slipped into depression at the lack of physical touch, not to mention the feelings of isolation and loneliness.

Hugs, handshakes, gentle touches of acknowledgement... All of these healthy forms of affection were taken away in light of the well-founded fear of spreading germs from a highly contagious virus.

My Latina friends really struggled with this. In that culture, you greet each other with an air kiss on the cheek. Women hug. Men shake hands and sometimes also hug. Every time someone arrives, he or she must greet every person in the room. And whenever you leave, give yourself more than a few extra minutes to get out the door because you must go back around again and kiss everyone goodbye.

"What I Really Need is a Kiss"

My Venezuelan friend had come to Colorado for a visit. This was one of the guys I had a crush on the first time I went to Venezuela, when I was eighteen. And I think a few mutual friends suspected something like that when he accepted their invitation to come for a visit to get to know the church there in Colorado.

Culturally, there are many differences between Latinos and North Americans. There are differences between a Southerner and a Bostonian, so you can imagine the culture shock that faced a Venezuelan who came to Colorado for a visit, in the winter.

He marveled at the snow, grateful for the layers of clothes, hat, coat, scarves, and gloves that we loaned him. Having grown up in the second hottest state in the tropical climate of Venezuela, he was not accustomed to the cold. The Rocky Mountains contrasted with the Andes. And the comparisons continued as he searched his mind to find a place to put all these strange, wonderful, new experiences.

"You know how to pump your own gas?" His eyes grew wide as he realized many small things that others never knew might be different. (In a cash-based culture like Venezuela, it is best for everyone if there are attendants to pump your gas, take your payment, and let you continue on your way.)

He joined in the Hispanic worship services, Bible studies, and other church activities, feeling a little more at home there, but he kept asking, "Where are the people?"

I finally realized what he meant, having been to Venezuela multiple times by then, "Where are the people *on the street?*" Owning a car in Venezuela is not as commonplace as it is in many regions of the U.S. Public transportation is more readily available and it is expected that you will walk to get to most of the places you need to go. Even if you are looking for a bus, taxi, or mass transit in a larger city, you are around crowds of people all the time and have the opportunity to interact with strangers or run into people you know. In many cities across the U.S., at least in Colorado, this is much less common.

Once we realized his desire to be around people as much as possible, we invited him to all activities of the church, in Spanish, in English, large gatherings, small gatherings, whatever.

I remember on one particular occasion, this time in English, we were all hanging out at the house where three of us lived, which doubled as a student center for middle school, high school, and college aged kids from church. After the youth devotional, he and I stayed seated on the couch along with a few others who stayed to hang out, but they later tired of the time it took for him to slowly practice his English or for me to translate back and forth. When they moved on to play games and eat, he and I remained chatting. The cultural differences between Venezuela and the U.S. came up again and he began to enumerate the other things he missed about his home country.

Coincidentally, in the middle of this part of the conversation, that moment of stark silence that can happen in a noisy crowd of people happened. He had been speaking quite loudly, as many Venezuelans do, but at that exact moment of the silence, he exclaimed, in perfect English, of course, "What I really need is a kiss!"

I have no doubt that I turned beet red as I quickly responded, equally loudly, "I understand how you miss the traditional Venezuelan greeting of a kiss on the cheek every time someone arrives or leaves."

By that point, the damage was done. I would never hear the end of the teasing that I should help a guy out and give him what he really wanted... a kiss!

He was innocently expressing his desire for physical affection, a rarer commodity in the culture he was visiting than in the one of his home country. But we all know that not all physical affection is as innocent nor as easy to resist.

Hierarchy of Needs or Priorities as God Designed Them?

On more than one occasion in my 40's, I shared classes and chapel talks with thousands of young women at Harding University on the topic of Singleness. Many girls, that day and for years afterward, approached me with various expressions of thanks for speaking in a positive way about something they rarely heard spoken of at all, or only occasionally as an afterthought.

After one such presentation, I had a booth in the Student Center sharing some of the women's ministry resources, Bible study materials, and mentoring opportunities through Iron Rose Sister Ministries (IronRoseSister.com). My dad was helping out in the background and had arrived to cover the bases while I went to eat my lunch. The specific detail about my dad's presence that day highlights the awkward nature of the conversation that was about to happen...

A young lady started to approach the table, then hesitated. Noting her reluctance, I leaned over and said, "Excuse me, did you have a question?"

Emboldened by my invitation, she walked closer. "Yes, I did. I was in the talk you gave, and I wondered if what you said was really true.

You didn't say it directly, but you implied that you are a virgin. Have you really never had sex? I was just wondering if that was even possible."

Slightly taken aback by her directness, but undaunted by her question, I responded, "Yes, it's true. I've never had sex. I've never been married."

"Oh, you don't have to be married to have sex," she retorted, shaking her head at my archaic thinking. She continued her comments with an impassioned explanation of her interpretation of the hierarchy of needs, "because sex is a primary one of our needs that must be met." She followed her emphatic statements with an invitation to download many of the different dating apps available so that I could, "hook up, no commitments, no strings attached... just meet that physical need and move on. Have you ever considered doing that?"

When she paused, awaiting my response, I briefly wondered what my dad was thinking, sitting behind me, but more important than his awkwardness was the opportunity to share truth with this young lady. "Well," I began, "I believe God designed sex to take place exclusively in the context of marriage. When a husband and wife have committed to each other before God and others, when they decide to become one, they enter into a union that is physical, emotional, mental, and spiritual. We are a whole being. Yes, sex is a physical act, but we can't detach it from the emotional, mental, and spiritual aspects of what sex involves. And when we try and make sex only physical or take it out of the context of that complete union, it deeply affects us, emotionally, mentally, and spiritually."

Still disagreeing with my statements, as evidenced by the constant head shaking and puzzled expression, she responded, "So you would really never have sex with anyone you aren't married to? I take it then you wouldn't live with someone and have sex to make sure everything works and that y'all are a good fit sexually?"

"Anatomically and hormonally speaking, God designed things to work when a man and a woman come together in sexual union."

"Yeah, but what if he wants sex way more often than she does or likes certain things and she doesn't? Shouldn't she make sure they are on the same page and are sexually compatible before they decide to get married?"

"I agree that they should talk through whether or not they believe they would be compatible partners before they enter into marriage, but partners in *every* aspect of life—not just sexually. Besides, even if they each think they're at a certain place right then, there is no telling what will happen during their lives—physically or emotionally or in whatever way—that changes the sexual and other dynamics in their relationship. But within marriage, they have made a commitment to navigate those things together."

"Yeah, I don't agree with you. And I still think you should check out [those apps] and hook up. You can't deny that need."

"Thank you for your suggestion, but I'm not going to do that. And, so you know, I'm not *ignoring* that need. It is more important to me to follow God's design for sex and for marriage instead of what you're suggesting. My commitment to Him and to His ways is a higher priority to me than that need, or any other need I might have."

"Well, thanks for answering my question. Good for you. Not everyone can do that. I certainly can't."

And with that closing remark, she walked away.

I turned around to my dad and said, "So, you heard all of that, huh?"

"Yep."

"Well, if you had any doubts before, now you know where I stand on the matter."

"Yep."

"I wasn't going to let the fact that you were sitting behind me stop me from having that conversation with her."

"I'm glad you didn't. She needed to hear all that."

Dad and I continued our conversation lamenting the fact that probably no one had ever had a conversation like that with her before that day. I was sad for her. I was sad for those I know who have followed a similar path she was on or was at least proposing. I was grateful that I had been able to plant a seed of truth. I never saw her again. And I never even got her name. But I have prayed for her.

I have prayed that she would know that inherent in God's love for her is His design and His purpose for her good. I have prayed that she would know that no matter what she has done sexually, or in other areas that have not been in line with God's design for His people, God still loves her and longs for her to come to Him (Luke 15).

I wish I had shared with her about God's hope of redemption. I wish I had shared about the blessing of forgiveness and how He wipes the slate clean. I wish I had told her about how many times God took Israel back after she had prostituted herself to other nations and even offered to call her virgin Israel (Jer. 31). I wish I had told her the painful and difficult love story of Hosea and Gomer that reminds us of God's love that extends beyond our betrayal.

Sisters, while I cannot rewind and go back to that conversation with the young lady who approached me in the Student Center, please let me speak those truths to you.

1. **God's love for you is unconditional, gracious, merciful, abundant, and never-ending.** (John 3:16; Rom. 8:31-39; 1 John 4:8-10; Lam. 3:21-24; Ps. 139)

2. **God wants what's best for you sexually, emotionally, mentally, physically, and in every single aspect of your life.** (Rom. 1:24-32; 2 Tim. 1:7; Rom. 12:1-2; Mark 12:1-12)

3. **God's plan and God's design really are best and are worth the sacrifices it may take to follow His plan and live in His design.** (Rom. 12:9-21; Is. 55:8-9; John 14:6; Gal. 5:13-26)

4. **No matter how far you have strayed from God's plan or His design... No matter how far you feel from God's love... No matter how unlovable you feel... God is calling you back to His arms of love and extending His invitation for repentance, forgiveness, and a life lived with Him made possible by the sacrifice of His Son.** (Ps. 32, 103:7-18; Hosea; Luke 15; Eph. 2:1-10; 1 John 1:5-10)

5. **When we live out our love for God and for others, our one single reason, it is easier to trust His ways and that He will truly give us the desires of our heart. He will transform the deepest desires of our heart to align with those of His heart.** (John 14:15-27; Prov. 3:5-6; Ruth)

Ladies, I invite you to ask God specifically to transform the desires of your heart. You can ask Him to align them with His desires. You can ask Him to clarify those desires and help you get to the heart, the underlying desire, even if, in that moment, you feel that the desire can only be fulfilled in one specific way or another. Ask Him if He has given you that desire or if Satan has introduced it in a way that is tempting or challenging you. Picture yourself entering the throne room and laying your desires at His feet. It may take several times of doing this before you are able to truly let them go and give them over to Him (1 Pet. 5:7). After you have fully expressed and completely handed over the desires of your heart to God, wait and see if, when, and how He gives them back to you. He will eliminate the desires that came from Satan. He will embellish and open the doors for desires that He has transformed, and He will fulfill them in ways that are beyond what you can ask or imagine.

Which of the biblical truths in the numbered list do you most need to hear?

Which of these truths do you most want to share with others?

Table Talk

While we recognize that the desire for physical affection exists, we cannot let it eclipse the deepest desires of our heart for deep relationship and for meaningful purpose. These are best fulfilled through the completion of the Greatest Command (Mark 12:29-31) and the Great Commission (Matt. 28:18-20).

God's desires for our lives are greater than our own personal desires. Prayer and depth of relationship with God will align our desires with His desires, over time. **By living out our first love for God, He will truly transform the desires of our heart (Ps. 37:4).**

Talk with God (Reflection Questions)

How does identifying the deepest desires of our heart relate to the conversation about "one single reason"?

Are there deep desires for relationship or for purpose that you feel are unfulfilled? You may be fervently asking God to answer those prayers or to transform the desires of your heart... or maybe you need to be lifting them up to God.

Is there a time in which you have experienced God transforming the desires of your heart—whether in relationship or in purpose? Make note of it as a reminder of His love for you and His provision.

Are you currently struggling with a longing for physical affection? Have you been able to pray about it and give it over to God, or is it something that has consumed you?

Talk with an Iron Rose Sister (Common Threads)

An area in which you want to grow or bloom

A thorn you'd like to remove (a hindrance from moving forward in this conversation or from fulfilling your purpose in God's Kingdom, an unhealthy desire)

An area in which you'd like to dig deeper or need someone to hold you accountable

---

Table Talk with One Another (one-on-one or group discussion)

What was your favorite verse in Isaiah 54 (pg. 77)?

Going back to Chapter 9 and the in-depth look at John 15 (pg. 80-82), what insights did you gain from that exercise about relationships and purpose?

What single woman's story can we celebrate as an example of deep relationship or meaningful purpose?

What is your reaction to the contents of these chapters about the transformation of our desires, our deepest desires for deep relationship and meaningful purpose, or our longing for physical affection? Please explain where you are coming from in your reactions. As you dialogue about this, be sure to listen, learn, and love one another, especially if there is something you agree with, disagree with, or would like to provide additional insight about from your own experience.

If you're willing, let's swap stories about one of the deepest desires of our heart. Has God fulfilled it, transformed it, or are you still waiting?

How has the topic of longings and desires impacted you? What makes this conversation important to you?

Can you describe for me an experience in which there has been healthy intimacy of relationship (e.g., an Iron Rose Sister who has served as iron sharpening iron in your life and encouraged you to be the best version of yourself, as God created you to be)?

How have your insights or perceptions changed after discussing aspects of this section with someone else?

Walk the Talk

What is one single **Action Step** you can take or next-step conversation to have with others?

How can we help facilitate deep relationships that fulfill meaningful purposes together in the Kingdom?

Tips for Small Group Table Talk

The biblical foundation of God's design for our relationships and our purposes should be the primary emphasis of these conversations. It can be easy to spend the entire time in discussion of relationship dynamics, sexual identity, or the challenges that come with a longing for physical affection. May we keep our eyes fixed on Jesus and remember our one single reason, as modeled by Christ.

Section IV

Avoiding the CAJE Traps

⁵ For this reason, when I could bear it no longer, I sent to learn about your faith, for fear that somehow the tempter had tempted you and our labor would be in vain... ⁶ But now that Timothy has come to us from you, and has brought us the good news of your faith and love and reported that you always remember us kindly and long to see us, as we long to see you... ¹² and may the Lord make you increase and abound in love for one another and for all, as we do for you. (1 Thes. 3:5-6, 12, ESV)

Expressions of frustration, rooted in comparisons, assumptions, judgements, and expectations were the common chorus to the refrains of each voice expressed through the surveys and interviews. The echoed sentiments, stemming from the commonality of these struggles, reverberated on the walls of these entrapping pitfalls.

These traps inherent in a conversation about singleness can cripple us from engaging in healthy conversation and limit our ability to relate. They can hinder the fulfillment of the deepest desires of our heart. When entrapped, our perceptions become clouded. Yet, love is the biggest and strongest tool in our arsenal to tear down the walls and break out of the entrapping cages.

CHAPTER 13

The CAJE Problem

¹In you, Lord, I have taken refuge; let me never be put to shame; deliver me in your righteousness. ⁴Keep me free from the trap that is set for me, for you are my refuge. (Ps. 31:1, 4, NIV)

I am fully aware of the misspelling, but please indulge me through this section in an effort to highlight the traps that encage us: CAJE. The CAJE of Comparisons, Assumptions, Judgements, and Expectations entrap and entangle, locking us in a "cage/caje" of our own creation and the accuser's design.

No one likes to be put in a box. References to someone as a caged animal are often warnings that he/she is about to lash out and attack. Proceed with caution! Our animal instincts kick in when we feel attacked or put in a stereotyped box of what it means to have never been married, to be separated, divorced, or widowed. Sometimes we sulk away silently and lick our wounds. Other times, we react and counterattack with a biting declaration of what the person can do with their comment. Or we use a sarcastic explanation to put ourselves on the offensive, even making fun of ourselves because self-inflicted wounds can be easier to handle than the wounds of others. Right? Um, no. All wounds hurt.

When we feel attacked or entrapped, whether by others or ourselves, we can feel especially alone. At those times, the book of Psalms has been of special comfort to me. David, the shepherd boy turned king, had experiences across his lifetime that provided frequent opportunities for him to cry out to God, expressing his frustrations. Some of those very psalms have been turned into songs that remind us of our ultimate source of help, the One who breaks the snare and invites us to escape into freedom (Psalm 124:7). Listen to the invitation in this psalm of ascent.

> **124** *If it had not been the Lord who was on our side— let Israel now say—*
> *⁶ Blessed be the Lord, who has not given us as prey to their teeth!*
> *⁷ We have escaped like a bird from the snare of the fowlers;*
> *the snare is broken, and we have escaped!*
>
> *⁸ Our help is in the name of the Lord,*
> *who made heaven and earth.* (Ps. 124:1, 6-8, ESV)

"We have escaped like a bird from the snare of the fowlers..." This imagery reminds me of Maya Angelou's poem "Caged Bird." [25] Using a vivid metaphor, she captures the plight and struggle of Blacks, suppressed by slavery. Angelou became a well-known voice during the American Civil Rights Movement of the 1960's, as her writings articulated the feelings of being oppressed, trapped, and encaged.

The expression of the caged bird singing was borrowed from the poem "Sympathy," by Paul Laurence Dunbar in 1899. [26] The final four lines of Dunbar's poem highlight the prayerful facet of the caged bird's song.

---

[25] The poem was first published in Angelou's book *Shaker, Why Don't You Sing?* by Random House in 1983. The poem is sometimes referred to by the full title, *I Know Why the Caged Bird Sings*, which is the title of her autobiography, originally published in 1969, republished in 1993 by Bantam Books.

[26] Dunbar, Paul Laurence, "Sympathy," in *Lyrics of the Hearthside*. (New York: Dodd, Mead and Company, 1899).

It is not a carol of joy or glee,
But a prayer that he sends from his heart's deep core,
But a plea, that upward to Heaven he flings—
I know why the caged bird sings!

Angelou continues her description of the caged bird's longings, primarily for freedom, contrasted by the free bird leaping, floating, and eating fat worms in earlier stanzas.

The caged bird sings
with a fearful trill
of things unknown
but longed for still
and his tune is heard
on the distant hill
for the caged bird
sings of freedom.

Can you hear the voices of the caged birds singing? It is not my intention to equate the struggles of single women with the oppression of many African Americans in the U.S. who have endured the burden of racism—the same racism that ushered in slavery. However, the cries of many underrepresented groups, especially in certain settings (like single women in many churches), can feel like caged birds singing. **And we want to hear their voices.**

Each of our stories are unique, but there exist many parallels in the traps we fall into because we have the same enemy that longs to encage our spirits.[27] The accuser wants to discourage us by the comparisons, assumptions, judgements, and expectations—our own and those of others.

Listening ears and loving hearts help us learn from one another and give everyone a voice in the conversation and a seat at the table. At

---

[27] These traps apply to everyone, no matter what our marital status.

such a table, we can celebrate our diversity and value every single person as a vital member of the body.

> *⁴There are different kinds of gifts, but the same Spirit distributes them.*
> *⁵There are different kinds of service, but the same Lord.*
> *⁶There are different kinds of working, but in all of them and in everyone it is the same God at work.*
> *¹²Just as a body, though one, has many parts, but all its many parts form one body, so it is with Christ. ¹³For we were all baptized by one Spirit so as to form one body—whether Jews or Gentiles, slave or free—and we were all given the one Spirit to drink. ¹⁴Even so the body is not made up of one part but of many.*
> (1 Cor. 12:4-6, 12-14, NIV)

Notice how many times the apostle Paul refers to many being one, differences coming together, distinctness being the same—all through the one Lord we serve and by whose Spirit we are guided. One body is made up of many parts and those parts cannot and should not be alike. With Christ as the head, we are each called to support one another in the body.

The church, as the body of Christ, has the opportunity to support every "single" member of the congregation. Jordan, a single woman missionary, recommends how we stay out of encaging traps...

> By viewing single women as having valuable experience and gifts that can be used to bless the body, but also not ignoring the differences. For example, including singles in retreats, teaching classes, and ministry activities of the church, but also, occasionally allowing separate single women's classes or activities that will address and encourage them in their differences.

Amen, Jordan! The apostle Paul continues with a similar encouragement that celebrates our differences and recognizes how much we need each other in the body. Let's finish reading 1 Corinthians 12:15-31 (NIV) as the text highlights each of the four CAJE traps: Comparisons, Assumptions, Judgements, and Expectations.

¹⁵Now if the foot should say, "Because I am not a hand, I do not belong to the body," it would not for that reason stop being part of the body. ¹⁶And if the ear should say, "Because I am not an eye, I do not belong to the body," it would not for that reason stop being part of the body. ¹⁷If the whole body were an eye, where would the sense of hearing be? If the whole body were an ear, where would the sense of smell be? ¹⁸But in fact God has placed the parts in the body, every one of them, just as he wanted them to be. ¹⁹If they were all one part, where would the body be? ²⁰As it is, there are many parts, but one body.

²¹The eye cannot say to the hand, "I don't need you!" And the head cannot say to the feet, "I don't need you!" ²²On the contrary, those parts of the body that seem to be weaker are indispensable, ²³and the parts that we think are less honorable we treat with special honor. And the parts that are unpresentable are treated with special modesty, ²⁴while our presentable parts need no special treatment. But God has put the body together, giving greater honor to the parts that lacked it, ²⁵so that there should be no division in the body, but that its parts should have equal concern for each other. ²⁶If one part suffers, every part suffers with it; if one part is honored, every part rejoices with it.

²⁷Now you are the body of Christ, and each one of you is a part of it. ²⁸And God has placed in the church first of all apostles, second prophets, third teachers, then miracles, then gifts of healing, of helping, of guidance, and of different kinds of tongues. ²⁹Are all apostles? Are all prophets? Are all teachers? Do all work miracles? ³⁰Do all have gifts of healing? Do all speak in tongues? Do all interpret? ³¹Now eagerly desire the greater gifts.

What happens when the eye **compares** herself with the hand?

What happens when the ear **assumes** that the foot is not part of the body?

Is it up to the internal organs to **judge** which external part is more necessary?

What about the **expectation** that in the body of Christ, your gifts would've been distributed differently? (e.g., "I thought I would be a mouth, but instead I'm a knee.")

Do you feel the bars of the CAJE closing in to trap us as we reflect on these questions?

Comparisons, assumptions, judgements, and expectations warp the perceptions of our identity. Furthermore, their traps keep us from fulfilling our role in the body and from rejoicing in the honor of the other parts' roles. **The CAJE distorts our perspective on our and everyone else's identity.**

Just as the CAJE can trip us up from moving forward in our own lives, it can blind us to the suffering another part is enduring (1 Cor. 12:26). When we recognize suffering, we long to comfort those with the same comfort we have received (2 Cor. 1:3-6). Yet sometimes the first step toward comfort and away from the shackles of the CAJE is to mourn alongside the other person or simply accompany her in her suffering (Rom. 12:15; Job 2:11-13, silent supporters who mourned with Job in his pain).

Be sure not to fall into a CAJE pity party!

What started as a noble desire to mitigate or explain away Job's pain turned into a disastrous trap that Job struggled not to fall into himself. Job's know-it-all friends assumed they knew more than they did—even than God did—comparing Job to others and passing judgement on their friend. As Job reminded all of us at the beginning of the book that shares his name, we cannot force our expectations on God, nor on others. Rather, God is to be praised and blessed in all circumstances.

*And he said, "Naked I came from my mother's womb, and naked shall
I return. The Lord gave, and the Lord has taken away; blessed be the name of
the Lord." (Job 1:21, ESV)*

The Lord has given, and the Lord has taken away in each of our lives. The pain is real, ladies. And for that, I am sorry. I hear you. I see you. You are loved. You are prayed for. And you are not alone. We want to hear your voice in this conversation.

Your voice may be one of current suffering, feeling ensnared by these traps. For other voices, the raspy tone is borne from the remnant scars of deep wounds caused, ultimately, by Satan's deceit and the damaging nature of sin. **While expectations may not necessarily be a sin, they join the chorus with comparisons, assumptions, and judgements in a disharmonious quartet of deception, conducted by the accuser himself.** We will NOT give him the last word. The deceiver has distorted things long enough. He has not one iota of love in his being. He has been permanently excused from the table, and his voice is no longer welcome in this conversation. Right?!

In contrast, God's melodious harmonies lift our spirits and unite our voices as a beautiful blending of every single identity found in Him. **Our finely tuned refrain echoes in the hearts of all those who have found their true selves by hearing the One voice that matters most.** He has called us by name, we are His (Is. 43:1). Seeing ourselves and one another through the lens of God's love is the only way we can move forward, freed from the CAJE.

Love God, love others, and love self. Look to God, keep our eyes fixed on Him, and the CAJE traps will lose their power over us.

As we are discovering, Prayer, Encouragement, Activities, and Reminders of Truth (PEAR) play their part in support of one another *and* serve as tools to break down the CAJE trap the accuser has set.

Yet the deceiver wants to turn those supportive, freeing tools into entrapping bars of the CAJE box. For example, **assumptions** may hinder us from **encouraging** someone that appears to be strong. **Comparisons** discourage us from impromptu **activities** that may not measure up to someone else's elaborately planned event. Satan's lies about how we are **judged** or how we judge ourselves overshadow **reminders of truth. Prayers** become whispers void of hope when our **expectations** remain unmet.

We are in this battle together, ladies! So, before we proceed, let's put on the armor of God (Eph. 6:10-18), protect our hearts (Prov. 4:23), and ensure that the God of Angel Armies is still seated at the head of the table. He goes to battle for us (Ex. 14:14) and He is the one guiding our conversation. **We will rely on the sword of His Word as a vital part of this and all our conversations.**

We will look at each of these traps individually and hear from various women and their stories. As we do, may we remember that 1 Corinthians 12 calls us to unity in Christ through the diversity of the body. In the final chapter of this section, "The CAJE Solution," we will come back to our one single reason and examine it through the very next chapter of the letter to the Corinthians (1 Cor. 13).

Love is the solution and our one single reason, no matter how intertwined or complicated the traps. Assumptions and judgements more often come from others and are therefore external pressures. The perceived pressure of comparisons and expectations tend to be internal CAJE traps. **All four traps are enhanced and intensified by our own internal monologues.**[28]

Don't be discouraged if you feel like you have already fallen (Ps. 145:14). We are here to help each other leave the CAJE behind, to forgive others we feel have encaged us, and to move forward in healing conversation. God's got this. Let's lean in and listen to the conversational insights from Him and from each other.

---

[28] In the survey responses, comparison traps were shared by everyone. Assumptions most often came into play for single women who have never been married. Judgements were most often mentioned by single-again women, whether from divorce or separation. And like comparisons, expectations came to bear for single and single-again women.

In light of those perceived external pressures, magnified by our internal thoughts, **this section speaks not only to single and single-again women but also to the church as a whole**. As the church, we want to walk and talk openly with one another to avoid the traps of Comparisons, Assumptions, Judgements, and Expectations.

CHAPTER 14

Comparisons

Two cows were grazing in a pasture when they saw a milk truck pass.
On the side of the truck were the words,
"Pasteurized, homogenized, standardized, Vitamin A added."
One cow sighed and said to the other,
"Makes you feel kind of inadequate, doesn't it?"[29]

From middle school to middle age, social media capitalizes on our insecurities. Another woman's highlight reel or her selfies with softening filters are not a true representation of what is going on in her life. **We are all broken, imperfect people.** And for women, our hormones tend to exacerbate the situation. Learning how to navigate our shifting hormones, especially during the teen years, can be especially challenging. Bethany describes the insecurities that characterize that stage of life.

There was a bit of insecurity between me comparing myself to other girls in high school. And that's a lot of what being a teenager is, that very scary egocentrism where you're just focusing on yourself and

---

[29] John Maxwell. Edward K. Rowell and *Leadership*, editors. *1001 Quotes, Illustrations, and Humorous Stories for Preachers, Teachers, and Writers* (Grand Rapids, Michigan: Baker Books, 2008).

you're like, "Everyone can see my flaws. This is terrifying. Everyone hates me." It's that natural worry as a young person, that stage of life...

Bethany's transparency about her struggles in high school, and later during college and beyond, helps us see that we are not alone in our way of thinking.

> ... and worrying that they're not sharing the things that I'm struggling with, so I feel like they might judge me if I say what I'm going through right now. When in reality, if I had... Later on, I learned they had dealt with that, too. Why didn't I say something then? Or why didn't they say something to me? Either way. But just learning that not everyone is perfect, and you don't need to compare yourself to others so much. **Because you don't know what everyone else has going on behind the scenes.**

The comparison trap fuels our competitive nature. And if we are all honest, especially when we have been hurt or feel like we don't measure up, we women can get mean. It can be a scary world out there among other women! Mean girls can make us feel unsafe and insecure. **A sense of confidence and security in Christ welcomes everyone to the table, honors the validity of each woman's story, and creates a safe space in which we can openly share.**

Open, honest communication and vulnerability can be scary, but they are necessary for us to be able to engage in genuine conversations. That kind of dialogue affords us the opportunity to sincerely support one another and serve as iron sharpening iron (Prov. 27:17).

When we fall into the trap of comparison, we forget that in comparison to Christ, we all fall short (Rom. 3:23, 6:23; James 2:10). When we recognize that none of us are perfect and that no one measures up without Christ's help, we can celebrate that only together in Him can we be made perfect or measure up.

[11] So Christ himself gave the apostles, the prophets, the evangelists, the pastors and teachers, [12] to equip his people for works of service, so that the body of

Christ may be built up ¹³until we all reach unity in the faith and in the knowledge of the Son of God and become mature, attaining to the whole measure of the fullness of Christ.

¹⁴Then we will no longer be infants, tossed back and forth by the waves, and blown here and there by every wind of teaching and by the cunning and craftiness of people in their deceitful scheming. ¹⁵Instead, speaking the truth in love, we will grow to become in every respect the mature body of him who is the head, that is, Christ. ¹⁶From him the whole body, joined and held together by every supporting ligament, grows and builds itself up in love, as each part does its work. (Eph. 4:11-16, NIV)

And did you see that love was listed as a vital piece of the support and growth process?

When I am filled by God's love and allow my identity to be defined by Christ, the head of the body, I can celebrate each part of the body growing and building itself up in love. I can rejoice in the work we each do instead of feeling twinges of jealousy when I compare my role in the body with someone else's.

The grass is always greener on the other side of the fence... Or is it? **Comparison is the enemy of contentment.** Even my sister's dog, that accompanied her when she stayed with my parents, decided that the food from my parents' dog's bowl tasted better than hers. And my parents' dog? You guessed it. He preferred food and water from the new bowls and complained when they were empty. Before there was another bowl for comparison, he had been perfectly content to eat from his own bowl. Silly dogs, we humans would never do that!

We do not dare to classify or compare ourselves with some who commend themselves. When they measure themselves by themselves and compare themselves with themselves, they are not wise. (2 Cor. 10:12, NIV)

In our heads, we know we shouldn't compare ourselves with others. We see the foolishness and destructive nature of the spiral we succumb to when we fall into that trap. And yet we do it, time and time again.

Think of the comparison traps Rachel and Leah fell into as the beautiful, beloved one, contrasted with the less-beautiful one who had all the children (Gen. 29-30). And speaking of kids, how was Hagar to compare herself to Sarah, the one to whom was given the promise, leaving Hagar as a single mom (Gen. 16:1-8)?

Women that have never married may identify with Leah in feeling like the less desirable choice or the one that has still not been chosen. You are loved, my single sisters. Single moms, remember that Hagar was the one who first called God, "The One who sees" (Gen. 16:13). He sees you in your struggles and you are not alone.

Listen to these excerpts of a blogger's story about the comparison between divorcees and widows.

> Unless you air your laundry, divorce in the church is as isolating as a child's temper tantrum during the Sunday morning service.
>
> When my husband of 27 years suddenly and unexpectedly left, it was weeks before my large-church-pastors noticed I was missing from Sunday morning services. And even weeks more before someone called to check in.
>
> I can't blame them. I didn't reach out. I was busy. I was inhaling and exhaling, managing shame, scrounging for hope, paying bills, and depositing what little emotional reserves I had to care for my devastated daughters, reeling family members, and befuddled friends. I was too busy facing the disappointment of opening my eyes in the morning, realizing that God hadn't granted my nightly plea to take me in my sleep because I didn't know how to live this way.[30]

Jill E. continues her description of the comparison between what a widow goes through and what a divorced woman goes through in their unique single-again experiences. Speaking in reference to a woman who was widowed shortly after Jill's divorce...

---

[30] Jill English, "The Casserole Rules," *Red Tent Living*, September 13, 2009, https://redtentliving.com/2019/09/13/the-casserole-rules/.

I love her and am grateful for each person who stepped in to meet her in her grief and need. One time, she gave me an extra casserole because her freezer was full. It was really tasty and I ate it for days after we wryly talked together about the differences in our experiences of the death of a marriage. We both acknowledged the casserole rules. The church didn't give divorce casseroles – except for the one she gave me.[31]

Comparison traps can lead to judgement traps if we are not careful. **Everyone could use a casserole.** We all have a need for support, for grace, and for freedom from the CAJE—whether it is of our own making or one that we perceive others to have imposed upon us. Listen to this commonly studied sister comparison and the way in which another sister entrapped herself by comparison and judgement for many years.

Sister Comparisons

Mary and Martha are often highlighted as the epitome of sister relationships. Luke 10:38-42 is the prime example, but when combined with John chapters 11 and 12, we gain additional insight into these two women.

> [38] *Now as they went on their way, Jesus entered a village. And a woman named Martha welcomed him into her house.* [39] *And she had a sister called Mary, who sat at the Lord's feet and listened to his teaching.* [40] *But Martha was distracted with much serving. And she went up to him and said, "Lord, do you not care that my sister has left me to serve alone? Tell her then to help me."* [41] *But the Lord answered her, "Martha, Martha, you are anxious and troubled about many things,* [42] *but one thing is necessary. Mary has chosen the good portion, which will not be taken away from her."*
>
> (Luke 10:38-42, ESV)

---

[31] Jill English, "The Casserole Rules," *Red Tent Living*, September 13, 2009, https://redtentliving.com/2019/09/13/the-casserole-rules/.

One Tuesday morning, after sharing a lesson and parts of my own story as a single woman in ministry, a widow approached me and confessed that she has always carried the guilt of being a Martha. She has heard the condemnation of Jesus' words in Luke 10 echo in her mind for her entire life. Mortified to hear her express the weight of this guilt, I reminded her of Martha's many attributes:

1. Martha opened her home to serve Jesus, even if she did get distracted (Luke 10:38).

2. Martha went to Jesus immediately upon hearing of His arrival after her brother Lazarus died, while Mary held back (John 11:20).

3. Amid her pain, and in contrast to her sister, Martha expressed her belief in Jesus and in the resurrection (John 11:21-27).

4. Martha invited her sister to engage with their friend Jesus and be comforted by Him (John 11:28).

5. Martha continued to serve Jesus (John 12:2).

Martha did none of these things perfectly. No one does. The comparison trap in Luke 10 makes Mary out as the better sister. John 11 leans the scale a little more in Martha's favor as the one to whom Christ revealed Himself as the resurrection and the life (John 11:25).

Whether we are distracted (Luke 10:40), or are struggling to believe because we are hurting (John 11:20, 28, 32), Jesus invites us to believe and to experience God's glory.

Then Jesus said, "Did I not tell you that if you believe,
you will see the glory of God?" (John 11:40, NIV).

Do you believe? Or maybe you feel that you are unworthy of that message being personally delivered to you? Imagine how Mary and Martha felt when Jesus, the Rabbi, took the time to teach two single women, whom He loved (John 11:5).

Jesus welcomes Martha, Mary, and every single woman to His table. We can sit at His feet and hear His voice speak truths over us.

We have been freed from the trap of comparison. Whether you identify with Martha, Mary, or maybe with their brother Lazarus who was resurrected, Jesus invites you to believe that you are His one single reason. Even if you were the only one on earth, God loves you enough to have sent His Son as an atoning sacrifice for your sins.

God values every daughter of the King and rescues her from any comparison trap. **We can walk freely in our identity shaped by His one single reason.**

CHAPTER 15

Assumptions

A gentleman in his nineties, after losing his wife of more than seventy years exclaimed, "This singleness is no joke! I thought people were just saying that stuff to get attention, but it is hard to be alone!"[32]

We get in big trouble when we assume. **One potentially paralyzing assumption is that we know what someone else is thinking or feeling.** Just ask the men in our lives, right? Well, remember the awkwardness no one died from back at the very beginning of this book? We may have to survive some awkward

---

[32] As stated by a friend of mine at church.

moments of sincere questions to engage in conversations that help us avoid the trap of assumptions.

The barista you befriend at the local coffee shop may appear to want nothing to do with Jesus, but when you get the full picture of her story, weeks after she has learned your regular order, what assumptions get thrown out the window? What do we assume when we see an unwed mother? How do those assumptions hurt our communication with her and our heart toward her?

Jesus loved to take people's assumptions and turn them around, shedding new light on an already established subject. "You have heard that it was said... But I tell you..." The Sermon on the Mount in Matthew chapters 5-7 is full of these examples. One of my favorites, as it applies to us single women, is found in Matthew 5:43-47 regarding our one single reason.

> *43 "You have heard that it was said, 'You shall love your neighbor and hate your enemy.' 44 But I say to you, Love your enemies and pray for those who persecute you, 45 so that you may be sons of your Father who is in heaven. For he makes his sun rise on the evil and on the good, and sends rain on the just and on the unjust. 46 For if you love those who love you, what reward do you have? Do not even the tax collectors do the same? 47 And if you greet only your brothers and sisters, what more are you doing than others? Do not even the Gentiles do the same? (ESV)*

It is easy to assume that someone else should have the responsibility of living out love to single women. Ladies, are we neglecting our own invitation and instruction, issued by Jesus? We each have a responsibility in this area. Every single person is called to live out love to the best of his/her ability.

My Own Assumptions Get Tested

After having worked with extensive populations of single women across the Americas, especially through church or ministry contexts, I entered my research (surveys and interviews) with a few theories to be tested. Most of my experiential observations were affirmed. However, a few assumptions were dismissed as categorical characterizations for single women.

One question in the survey was whether the single or single-again woman wanted to marry. I offered three options for their answer: "No, thanks," "Maybe" or "Yes, please!" My assumption was that the women would identify with one of those three answers and be able to make a selection. Yet many women bristled at my attempt to simplify such a complex question and neatly divide it into those three categories. More than a dozen of the 220 women referenced that question in their comments, clarifying her answer by expressing the question's difficulty, or providing better alternatives for the answer choices.

In the statistical analysis of the three answer choices, regarding their desire to marry, the strongest correlations were their age, their expressed level of contentment in their singleness, whether she was a parent, whether she had been married previously, and her home language.[33]

Younger women were more likely to answer "Yes," to wanting to get married, while older women were more likely to answer, "Maybe." The more content the woman in her singleness, the less likely she was to choose, "Yes, please," as her answer.

Most single women who are parents responded that they "Maybe" want marriage, while most women who are not parents responded that they would like to get married. Finally, the single women who had never married previously were more likely than the single-again to choose, "Yes, please," in response to their desire to marry.

While the percentage of Spanish-speaking women that expressed a desire to get married was higher than the percentage of English-

---

[33] Additional details and statistical data are available at https://IronRoseSister.com/single/

speaking women, **there were less differences between the two language groups across the rest of the questions than I anticipated.**

While the cultural setting may change the tone of the conversation or the specific context in which the topic of singleness is addressed, the underlying needs, perceptions, traps, and challenges were more paralleled than contrasting in each of the participants' answers.[34]

It reminded me of the struggles we all share as Christians. **Every single person strives to live out love, our one single reason, in our distinct circumstances.** The timeless truths in Scripture that speak to all of our struggles, no matter what our situation, affirm the living and active nature of the Word of God (Heb. 4:12). What a mighty God we serve! And I love that His love reaches every single one of us, meeting us where we are and inviting us into relationship with Him. He loves us and longs to engage in communication with us.

Communication... we are back to the importance of the dialogue in which we can authentically engage when we all come to the table. The overwhelming response in every woman's survey and/or interview was an appreciation that their voices were heard and that, through this book, I might serve as a voice that represents their own—for hearing their stories, and for bringing this often-avoided topic to the conversation.

It is my prayer for you, my single sisters, that you find and hear yourselves on the pages of this book. I pray that you are equipped to help others know how to have these vital conversations, even when

---

[34] Of course, distinctions played out more in the open-ended questions that highlighted the nuances of context and environment (qualitative responses) rather than in the data that could be analyzed (quantitative responses). There are a select number of factors that can be objectively quantified—factors that contribute to perceived support and acceptance (internal and external). While the nature of many struggles was the same, the intensity or the environment of those pressures may come from different sources (family, church, friends, society, etc.).

they're awkward, to break down assumptions, and to take the next steps toward love and healing.

If you are married and reading this, we thank you for coming to the table! Please help us break free from mistaken assumptions we have made about you, as well.

Through the pages of the Bible and through the testimonies of others, God invites us to break down the assumption walls of the CAJE and find freedom in the mutual love He provides and that we have for Him.

God Flips Assumptions on Their Heads

God honors His promises, but in His timing, in His way. Our assumptions about how He will fulfill them can get us into a lot of trouble. Naomi (pleasant) wanted her name changed to Mara (bitter) because of how forgotten she felt by God, how painful her experience was as a widow in a foreign country, and how unredeemable her situation seemed (Ruth 1:20-21). She assumed God had given up on her and her family. But God...! Remember that phrase? **It is never a good idea to assume we know what God is working on behind the scenes.**

God loves to use the least likely candidate to bring Him glory and honor. He selected the youngest of Jesse's children to be king and to bring salvation through his family line. David was a man after God's own heart, but the shepherd boy was small, not head and shoulders above the rest, like his predecessor, King Saul. And even after God had told David that He wanted to make him king, David had to wait for many years and through many trials (including multiple attempts on his life) to see that promise come to fruition. He's not the only one.

David? That small boy who thinks he's going to defeat a nine-foot-tall giant? No way.

Michelle Goff? That single girl, never married, who thinks she's going to conquer these giant insecurities in her life? No way.

\<Your name\>? That woman who thinks (whatever false assumption the accuser wants you to believe)? No way.

But God! The Almighty helped David defeat Goliath with one small stone in a slingshot to his head.

But God! The Great Comforter led Michelle to face her fears and be used as His instrument to launch Iron Rose Sister Ministries when she answered like Isaiah, "Here am I, send me!" (Is. 6:8).

But God! I invite you to claim and proclaim at least one "But God!" part of your story.

When we celebrate the God stories in our lives, we fly free from the CAJE traps. Even if an encaging assumption discourages us, we can break out from under its hold and radiate God's love that frees the other person from the CAJE of their own false assumption (Ps. 40:1-3).

Assumptions of a Seven-year-old

A precocious seven-year-old came to my house for a meal along with her family and other friends. She immediately asked me where the other children were. *Gulp.* When I responded letting her know that she and her sibling would be the only children with us that day, she looked puzzled.

I promptly showed her the tub of toys, the shelves of children's books, and other kid-friendly things about my house. Undaunted and undistracted in her mission, she attempted a different approach. She asked where the kids stay when they come to my house.

"Are your kids just gone and already big?" None of my answers were satisfactory to her seven-year-old mind. The possibility that I did not have children did not compute in her young brain.

When I explained that I am "the fun aunt" to my sister's children and to many of my friends' kids, she responded, "Oh, I have aunts, but they have their own kids."

Thankfully, mercifully, the timing of this conversation was at a point in my life when I was already at peace with my lack of children in the traditional sense. Twinges of past pain echoed in my mind, but I pushed them aside, replacing them with the joy of hosting a large meal with diverse individuals and remembering the spiritual children I know I have.

Flash back a few years prior to this conversation and insert a different version of the same questions and doubts. At that time, they crushed me; they discouraged me, deflated me, and allowed Satan to get a major foothold of discontent. I longed to have what others had: children.

It was always easier for me to imagine myself as a mom than as a wife. Remember the story about my transformed desires? When little girls would crown their heads with a pillowcase and pretend it was the veil as they marched down the hallway, I preferred to "nurse" the baby dolls or carry my sisters around on my nonexistent hips.

To the single moms reading this book, your longing may mirror that of the young girls with pillowcases. The big wedding forgotten, you long for a life partner with whom to share the responsibilities of raising a child. Or, having been burned and betrayed by one whom you thought was that life partner, you struggle to not let bitterness and distrust consume you.

Whether the innocent questions of a seven-year-old or the well-meaning comments of a grandma who "just wants you to be happy," the way in which others react to our current life state affects us. Those from whom we might seek support can be the greatest sources of disparaging remarks, especially when coupled with their errant assumptions.

False Assumptions

Open mouth, insert foot. We have all experienced a moment in which we wish we could rewind and un-say whatever thing just came out of our mouths. Here are a few examples of things that have been said—false assumptions—that have been especially hurtful to both women who have never married and to women who find themselves being single again (as quoted from surveys and interviews).

- All singles are selfish.

- Only those acting desperate for a husband long to marry.

- Singleness is all fun and games, freedom, and independence.

- Singles don't get exhausted, stressed, or overwhelmed.

- Marriage will solve all her problems.

- Only singles struggle with feeling lonely.

- Marriage is a promise, a rite of passage, and a requirement for Kingdom value.

- If a woman is pursuing a career, she doesn't want to get married.

- All single women have had sex.

Not all false assumptions are made by others about singles. Many single women make assumptions about how others see them or have their assumptions about other singles, as well. One can feel as if an eye of judgement is on you, but these assumptions we make about others are as encaging a trap as assumptions being made about us. No one is exempt from the Assumption CAJE.

Allison bristled every time someone assumed that she wanted to get married. She has fostered eleven children and adopted one, but never had a desire to get married.

After interviewing Kari A., a single-again mom, she expressed thanks for being able to talk openly about her story and relayed an assumption that many make.

> It was so good to be able to share part of my story. It was not all bad. Some of my best adventures and experiences were while I was married. And because people don't want to talk about the divorce, they think that it wipes out all of the rest of my past before the divorce, as well.

Do you assume someone wants to share her story? Or that she is ready to talk about her struggles? Do you assume you know the whole story?

In addition to offering a PEAR in support (Section II), radical human presence—just being there—is one of the best things we can do. It is also important, with your very being, to create a safe space in which the other person can feel supported and free to choose whether she talks about the most vulnerable aspects of her life.

Independence

The woman who leans on God and develops strong inner strength to face life as a single woman, out of necessity and design, becomes fiercely independent and self-sufficient. This independence can be seen as a strength, but it is also intimidating.

There is a two-edged sword or dichotomous challenge regarding independence. Fierce independence and self-sufficiency may be a by-product of being single, never married. The very things we must do to survive/thrive are perceived as threatening or intimidating.

And while strength and independence are attractive to many men, there are challenges to two independent individuals building a life together. Shaya affirms these dynamics.

> I am single and loving it.... there isn't really any "mostly" after that. When I answer "maybe" to getting married, that is only because if

God ever put someone in front of me who made my life more fun and allowed me to serve Him better, then I would consider getting married. But, at the age of 37, I actually feel it would be very difficult and scary to have to change my ways for another person. Maybe 2-3 times a year I get a little lonely and feel it would be nice to have a partner or spouse... it's usually when I want to travel (which I do love doing myself, but would like to do with someone I really liked too) or when I wish I had mine and my spouse's income to knock out my student loans. Haha! But other than that, I'm good! I always tell people my dream job is to be a stay-at-home mom with no husband and no kids. (I'm still figuring out how to make this happen!)

Shaya's story addresses several false assumptions. Susan continues with similar points.

In fact, the air quoted "time," is an assumption that as a single woman I have more time to give. That I should be able to be more involved in church activities or be able to give for this and that because my resources... I have more expendable resources. That's an assumption that may or may not be true.

Another assumption that I think is often associated with the life situation that I experience is that it's a choice. And in some ways, it is a choice, but in many other ways, it's the path that God has directed me down. From a younger perspective, there's an assumption that if you're not married by this point in your life then there must be something wrong with you. And I would suggest that is an incredibly false assumption and even a harmful assumption. I try to speak truth to that lie that Satan gives us by saying, 'God is faithful.' He makes me whole. **There is not something that is inherently wrong with me that has caused me to be single in my adult life. And yet, that assumption persists because Satan likes that lie.**

Being single and independent can create misconceptions about a single woman's desire for dependence on others. One single sister, never married, shared:

I fully recognize that I am perhaps independent to my detriment at times. But I wonder if sometimes my independence has been a coping mechanism and a result of the fact that I haven't always been supported in the ways that I've needed. That I've had to become independent in certain ways out of necessity.

"I've got this! But can you help me?" Inner strength is a necessity. Weakness and vulnerability are perceived to be an invitation to get hurt or taken advantage of. Self-sufficiency is a developed skill for a single woman and must be relearned by a woman who finds herself single again. Navigating a newfound independence, whether through divorce or widowhood is a challenging endeavor.

We are invited into a more intimate dependence on God. **Without God's guidance, we fall into the trap of an assumed identity.** When our life circumstances do not fit into the "norm" of a preconceived identity model, assumptions run rampant as we search for a point of connection to our known realities. And since singleness has not been normalized in many settings, one must make an extra effort to create a new mental pathway for this unique person, or for ourselves.

"You know my name, not my story. You've heard what I've done, not what I've been through," shared by a young, divorced sister.

Many assumptions about single and single-again women are made because our "normal" identity descriptors don't have a specific name or category for every story. **One inherent fallacy of assumptions is a lack of open communication—with God and with others.** When we offer others a seat at the table and come together in prayer, asking God to lead our conversations, we can break down our ill-conceived assumptions and, instead, build relationships of understanding. Ignorance is the breeding ground for assumptions. **In order to break down assumptions, we must engage in conversation that leads to the necessary knowledge, understanding, and wisdom.**

The more we live out our one single reason, the more God leads us with wisdom to know how to navigate these conversations.

IV: AVOIDING THE CAJE TRAPS • 143

Unfortunately, wisdom is not an automatic download of immediate direction to know how to eliminate false assumptions and navigate a new path forward. It is a process. However, God does promise that if we ask, He will give us wisdom (James 1:5).

Conversations with God and conversations with others will help us gain a deeper understanding of our erroneous assumptions. The more we understand, the more we can help normalize conversations about singleness—its blessings, its benefits, its challenges, and its truths.

Once we set aside our assumptions, we can more easily step into a "judgement-free zone" as we continue the conversation. What are some assumptions you have made about single or single-again women?

CHAPTER 16

Judgements

A woman was interviewed by reporters on her 102nd birthday. When asked about the benefits of living past the century mark, she answered, "No peer pressure!" [35]

---

[35] Win Arn in Edward K. Rowell and *Leadership*, editors. *1001 Quotes, Illustrations, and Humorous Stories for Preachers, Teachers, and Writers.* (Grand Rapids, Michigan: Baker Books. 2008), 293.

J udgements: such a heavy word that comes with its own baggage. Even the definitions feel burdened by our past experiences, filled with painful feelings and defining moments.

One type of judgement is the exercise of discernment. We make judgement calls to determine if something is right or wrong. It is the process of forming an opinion or evaluation by discerning and comparing. This is the way in which judgements can and should be used in healthy ways. We can call them **discerning observations**.

For example, Iron Rose Sisters, or Christians in general, make a commitment to follow Christ, to walk in His steps, to obey His Word, and to live as He calls us to live. Part of this commitment is to serve as accountability partners with one another as we each imperfectly allow ourselves to be transformed more and more into the image of Christ (2 Cor. 3:18). Along the way, if someone sees me start slipping into darkness, but I don't recognize that I am no longer walking in the light (1 John 1:5-10), I want someone to gently let me know that they have made these discerning observations. In those situations, an honest, loving conversation, out of concern for a Christian sister can help her become aware of the error and invite her to return to the light (John 3:16-21).

Nonverbal cues, context, timing, and tone are important. How the messenger delivers a message can be more significant than the message itself, especially when it is a discerning observation. If we can hear the truth spoken in love (Eph. 4:15), we have an opportunity to be set free through iron sharpening iron. If we hear everything through a distrusting filter of condemnation, we are doomed to stay encaged. Either way, our own defensiveness can be what entraps us more tenaciously than the perceived judgement itself. Our internal messages of self-judgement and self-doubt only serve to dig a deeper hole—a CAJE from which we feel we can never escape.

The statements or implied remarks that we get most defensive about are usually the areas in which we are already sensitive. They are either a sore subject and painful area of struggle, or an area in which we are aware that we are doing something wrong. In the case of the latter, the internal discernment/judgement bells have been sounding their alarm. Ignoring those warning nudges from the Spirit, we prefer to lash out and react to the messenger than to see the element of truth in their message. And for the painful remarks that touch an already sore subject, we may be falsely assuming the other person's harmful intent. What someone intends as a discerning, loving warning is perceived as the second type of judgement (detailed below).

Nevertheless, we can remember that God's arm is not too short to save (Is. 59:1). He longs to remind us of His one single reason and that He is big enough to redeem any errors of judgement—our own or someone else's. This world is only temporary. The One who conquered death invites us to a life of victory, freed from this mortal and perishable body in which we can so easily become entrapped.

54 When the perishable puts on the imperishable, and the mortal puts on immortality, then shall come to pass the saying that is written:

"Death is swallowed up in victory."
55 "O death, where is your victory? O death, where is your sting?"

56 The sting of death is sin, and the power of sin is the law. 57 But thanks be to God, who gives us the victory through our Lord Jesus Christ. (1 Cor. 15:54-57, ESV)

Amen!

The other type of judgement is critical condemnation, expressed toward Christians and non-Christians. It is the type of judgement that Jesus warns against in the Sermon on the Mount in Matthew 7.

7 "Judge not, that you be not judged. 2 For with the judgment you pronounce you will be judged, and with the measure you use it will be measured to you. 3 Why do you see the speck that is in your brother's eye, but do not notice the log that is in your own eye? 4 Or how can you say to your brother, 'Let me take the speck out of your eye,' when there is the log in your own eye? 5 You hypocrite, first take the log out of your own eye, and then you will see clearly to take the speck out of your brother's eye. (ESV)

Psalms 50, 58, and 75 speak about God judging with equity all peoples and nations. He is the ultimate Judge and we do not have that authority. Moses got that confused when he started to exact judgement on the Egyptians (Ex. 2:11-15; Acts 7:23-36). It is easy, like it was for Moses and many others, to think we are helping when what is communicated is filled with judgement.

"You don't measure up," is the message often received when a comment is being made to a single or single-again sister, even if it is not stated with a spirit of condemnation.

"¹³ Therefore let us not pass judgment on one another any longer, but rather decide never to put a stumbling block or hindrance in the way of a brother."
(Rom. 14:13, ESV)

How we communicate matters. As you have likely experienced, even when we are careful and prayerful, we may have left the other person feeling judged or condemned—the second type of critical judgement—through our words, attitudes, actions, or tone of voice. At those times, it is important for us to reiterate the love we have for that Christian sister and her well-being.

Only God knows our heart and our motivation for bringing up the topic. Check for the log before pointing out the speck. Talk with God at length before talking with your Christian sister about it. God will guide you regarding what to say, how to say it, when to say it, and whether or not to bring it up. **There is a way to point something out without pointing a finger.**

¹² Speak and act as those who are going to be judged by the law that gives freedom, ¹³ because judgment without mercy will be shown to anyone who has not been merciful. Mercy triumphs over judgment. (James 2:12-13, NIV)

Judgement CAJE Traps

Judgements of both types can feel like the pink elephant in the room—and I hate pink. Let's prayerfully and carefully navigate the conversations about the pink elephants and avoid the CAJE traps together. The weight of the judgement CAJE is overwhelming whether the judgements are expressed, implied, acknowledged, or simply anticipated. The accuser capitalizes on any type of judgement to keep us entrapped, burdened, and entangled in a false identity based on that judgement.

Judgements are a mistaken way to define our identity. We cannot allow the deceiver to get a foothold, nor let us believe a lie. Perceived judgements can be a catalyst for our own internal judgements. Comments become triggers for our own spiraling thoughts. When this happens, we can be the hardest on ourselves. As Kari A., a divorced single mom, quoted her counselor, "She reminded me just to put the stick down and stop beating myself up with it." Kari continued,

> You just kind of feel like a complete failure because you're just like, wow. You know, this is not how I dreamed my life to be. I was going to be this great wife, and I wasn't. I was going to be this great mom, and I don't know if I have been. I've been a decent mom, but you know... It's just the way it worked out.
>
> [After a meeting with the elders/shepherds of my congregation], I said, "It's like it usually takes two people to get into this mess." And one of the shepherds said, "Not always." I'm like, "Well, there are things I could have done better." He responded, "Well, we could all do things better."

We can all do things better. We are all a work in progress.

If we don't accept God's grace, the strongest critique of judgement may come from within ourselves. We can be our own worst enemies when it comes to the internal monologue filled with self-deprecation, self-doubt, and a hefty serving of Satan's lies and direct attacks.

In the story of Job, we recognize that Satan asked God if he could test Job (Job 1:6-12, 2:1-7). The greater test may not have come from the loss itself, but rather from the unsupportive comments by Job's friends. They excelled at the judgement facet of the CAJE.

11 Then Zophar the Naamathite answered and said: ² "Should a multitude of words go unanswered, and a man full of talk be judged right?"
(Job 11:1-2, ESV)

In verses 13-16 of Job 11, Zophar continues his rebuke of Job by assuming that Job has not fully devoted his heart to God. If you'll only do this... or that... If you only would repent from your sinful ways... Zophar's implied judgement is that Job has spoken out of turn and that surely Job has sinned and therefore God is punishing him for that sin.

Job's response in the following chapter reminds me that we are not alone in our frustrations when we feel that someone has taken an attitude of superiority toward us.

³ But I have understanding as well as you; I am not inferior to you.
Who does not know such things as these?
⁴ I am a laughingstock to my friends;
I, who called to God and he answered me,
a just and blameless man, am a laughingstock.
⁵ In the thought of one who is at ease there is contempt for misfortune;
it is ready for those whose feet slip. (Job 12:3-5, ESV)

When we feel like the laughingstock, the butt of jokes, "the one who never married," "the divorcee," or whatever other label of judgement we feel sentenced to, Job's declarations through the rest of Job 12 remind us that God is ultimately in charge.

God gets the last word on any judgement. Who and what He decides to bind will be bound and those He chooses to loose will be freed. In the same way that we celebrated how God flips assumptions on their heads, we can delight in the erroneous judgements that God dismisses like a vapor.

Unless we allow God to put them in perspective, external judgements, implied or implicit, are encaging. They can come in the form of rebukes, critiques, a scolding, passive/aggressive remarks, or a direct condemnation.

One single sister expressed frustration at another church member's judgement on her choice for higher education. "Why are you getting your Ph.D.? Honey, no man will ever marry you now!"

When assumptions become a passing of judgement, the words become painful. For example, comments that Courtney M. has heard have been especially discouraging as she lives out love in service to many young people through children's and youth ministries.

> The implication that I am a selfish person, and I don't know what love is because I am not loved by a man, and I don't have someone else to take care of—be it a husband or a child.

Judgements presented as disparaging comments are damaging, especially when they keep us at arm's length from someone who is hurting and in need of support. Carol is grateful for God's help, but wishes she had received support from her church as well.

> I was mother to a 9-month-old baby girl when my husband left us. Shortly after that I lost my job. My ex went to the church I was attending and convinced them he was willing to start over, but he was an alcoholic. They turned against me, so I had to make a completely new start. Uphill all the way. Learned a lot. Fought hard. But with God's help, made it.

We don't always know the full story. **Don't judge a book by the chapter you walked into the middle of.**

Bethany describes how many passed judgement on her mom after her divorce. They neglected to get the whole story and her mom was flooded with doubt during the entire process. She knew [divorce] was something she didn't want, and that God wasn't pleased with, but she also knew how destructive the marriage was for her personally, and for her three daughters.

But also, something my mom faced a lot after their divorce was people looking down on them because of it, or just judging them, or you know. And some people preaching, oh yeah, divorce is the worst thing ever. Don't do it. Make it work. Well, what if... There are certain things that are stated in scripture, like you're in this situation? No, get out. That's not ok. Marriage shouldn't exist when that is happening because that's not a real marriage. So, I think that should be spoken about more accurately, more truthfully. **Because when you talk about [divorce] so harshly and inaccurately that way, it hurts people.** That hurt my mom to hear those things.

I know there were times at least early on when she wondered, "Was this the right choice? Should we have gone this route? I don't know." But then ultimately, there was one day we were just... I think it was the first day my dad was out of the house, and we were just cleaning up around the house together. Just cleaning the house, and apparently – I don't remember this – I was the one who was like, "This has been the best day ever!" Just cleaning the house, doing something that shouldn't be fun. But it was the first day my dad wasn't there. And I said it was the best day ever, and my mom was like, "Ok, that's the closure I needed. I made the right choice. We're going to be ok."

We have a choice. We can listen to the critiques and remain encaged, or we can listen to Jesus acknowledge who we are and what we are trying to do. In Mark 14, we find the story of a woman who honored Jesus by anointing Him in the midst of others' criticism of her.

³And while he was at Bethany in the house of Simon the leper, as he was reclining at the table, a woman came with an alabaster flask of ointment of pure nard, very costly, and she broke the flask and poured it over his head.

⁴There were some who said to themselves indignantly, "Why was the ointment wasted like that? ⁵For this ointment could have been sold for more than three hundred denarii and given to the poor." And they scolded her.

⁶But Jesus said, "Leave her alone. Why do you trouble her? She has done a beautiful thing to me. ⁷For you always have the poor with you, and whenever you want, you can do good for them. But you will not always have me. ⁸ She has done what she could; she has anointed my body beforehand for burial. ⁹ And truly, I say to you, wherever the gospel is proclaimed in the whole world, what she has done will be told in memory of her."

(Mark 14:3-9, ESV)

Jesus came to the woman's defense despite the judgement being mounted against her. He saw her and valued her, recognizing that she had done what she could, and honoring her by stating that her story will be told in her memory. Her legacy was one of honoring Christ. She did not let the judgements of others encage her or hinder her from her task. She kept her focus and lived out her one single reason. Jesus returned the favor and showed her love at a vulnerable time, under the perusal of the onlookers.

For the "broken-hearted woman" who is facing divorce or separation, Kaitlyn affirms she is in greater need of support than condemnation.

> I believe the church has an especially difficult time showing support for the single-again woman, meaning divorced woman. The first thing I was asked after my divorce was if I had a "biblical reason" for it. Meaning did he commit adultery because that is the only way it is not a sin to get divorced. Instead of ensuring that the freshly broken-hearted woman is "biblically correct" or in need of condemnation herself by your human standard/understanding, why not ensure you are loving her as Jesus would have?

When the apostle Paul describes God's righteous judgement in Romans 2, his language leaves no room for doubt about the One in whose hands lie the just judgement. None of us is perfect and when we fall into the judgement CAJE—passing judgement on ourselves or on others—we are practicing the very things that we condemn. *"For in passing judgment on another you condemn yourself, because you, the judge, practice the very same things"* (Rom. 2:1b, ESV).

It can be easiest to pass judgement in the same areas in which we struggle. We most easily recognize our own faults and fears in others. Instead, we must forgive ourselves and forgive others. But did you know that forgiveness depends on one person and that reconciliation takes two? God has given us free will and, sometimes, an erroneous judgement comes when a sister is suffering the consequences of someone else's choices.

However, ladies, if we are suffering the consequences of our own decisions, let's avoid the self-deprecating comments. They are an ineffective defense mechanism and a lie. God's grace means that we are freed from the condemnation or punishment. There is a difference between natural consequences and punishment. Thankfully, when we repent and accept God's grace, He can cleanse even our consciences (Heb. 10:22).

It is for freedom that Christ has set us free (Gal. 5:1). And if we have repented and accepted God's loving grace through His Son, there is no longer any condemnation for us (Rom. 8:1)!

¹¹ Do not speak evil against one another, brothers. The one who speaks against a brother or judges his brother, speaks evil against the law and judges the law. But if you judge the law, you are not a doer of the law but a judge. ¹² There is only one lawgiver and judge, he who is able to save and to destroy. But who are you to judge your neighbor? (James 4:11-12, ESV)

The language in Isaiah 33:22 reminds us that our Judge is also our King and the One who will save us. *"For the Lord is our judge; the Lord is our lawgiver; the Lord is our king; he will save us."* (ESV)

CHAPTER 17

Expectations

*We must be willing to get rid of the life we've planned
so as to have the life that is waiting for us. –Joseph Campbell*[36]

No one expected Nehemiah, a humble cupbearer, to rebuild the wall of Jerusalem in 52 days, especially in light of such strong opposition.

No one expected Daniel and his friends to be stronger and healthier than the other young men after following a diet of vegetables and water for ten days instead of eating the king's food (Dan. 1:8-16).

No one expected Hananiah, Mishael, and Azariah to walk out of the fire unsinged, not even smelling of smoke. The best part of this surprisingly unfulfilled expectation is the answer given to the king in response to his command that they worship him or be thrown in the fire.

[17] If we are thrown into the blazing furnace, the God we serve is able to deliver us from it, and he will deliver us from Your Majesty's hand. [18] But even if He does not, we want you to know, Your Majesty, that we will not serve your gods or worship the image of gold you have set up. (Dan. 3:17-18, NIV)

---

[36] *A Joseph Campbell Companion: Reflections on the Art of Living*

"But even if He does not..."

God has the ability to do beyond what we can ask or imagine (Eph. 3:20). Amazingly, that power is at work within us, but it is not for our benefit or blessing. Rather, *"to him be glory in the church and in Christ Jesus throughout all generations, forever and ever. Amen"* (Eph. 3:21, ESV).

I want God to save my marriage, but even if He does not... to Him be the glory.

I want God to send me a husband. But even if He does not... to Him be the glory.

I expected that God would've given me more time with my husband, but even though He didn't... to Him be the glory.

I expected to have children by this point in my life, yet even though I haven't... to Him be the glory.

What is something you know that God is capable of doing but has not been brought about?

What is our response to this unmet expectation? To God be the glory.

For Elizabeth, the fact that her dreams and expectations have not matched up with the expected norm has been confusing for others—and even for her. Yet through it all, she has sought to give God the glory.

> My life has looked so different from the typical young woman who has grown up in the fellowship of the churches of Christ and gone off and been educated, and then worked in a career... and then married and had children... Because my life doesn't look like that, it's confusing [for others]. And I get that because in some ways it's also confusing for me! Like, "Why does my life *not* look like that?" But who am I to ask that question? **Because my question that I have to be asking is, "How is my life reflecting Christ? How am I serving His will on this earth?"**

Which may or may not mean being married and having children, having biological children, I should say. So, I guess in terms of the experiences that I've had in those different congregations, that's seemed to be a common theme: finding community but still having to deal with being a bit of an outsider within that community because my life doesn't look exactly like the expectation.

Elizabeth has strived to maintain a clear vision of her one single reason. Her love for Christ and for others has moved to the top of her priority list as she reframes her expectations.

It's not the life I imagined for myself, but throughout my adult life, I have regularly had to reimagine what life looks like and dream in ways that I look for opportunities to fulfill God's requests of us—to do the things that we are doing for His glory.

She has had to rely on God more, especially when her expectations for life didn't match up with the path He has directed her down.

Many times, our expectations don't match up, but this is the same God who transforms the desires of our heart. **God can redirect our expectations and clarify them through the lens of His eternal plan.**

"Grow up and marry a Christian man"

As a part of the evening routine, we would read a book and say our prayers. Every night, amidst the prayers of thanksgiving and various requests, my mom prayed over me and my sisters, "Please help her grow up and marry a Christian man." I can still hear my or my sister's childlike voices of faith echoing that prayer when it was our turn to verbalize the bedtime prayers. "De-uh God, pweze hep me gwow up and mawy a Cwistian man."

I do not fault my parents for the seed being planted of the priority of it being a Christian man if we were to marry, but the expectation was definitely there, as affirmed in society and in the church, that we would marry. The assumption was clear, and the expectation defined.

My mom cringes at the memory of these prayers and what they implied. I have long-since forgiven her and released her of any burden of responsibility she feels for the expectations that came with those prayers.

The beautiful thing is that her prayers have transformed to requesting "partners in the gospel" (Phil. 1:5). My partners in the gospel have spoken different languages, lived in different countries, shared different experiences, and through it all have taught me a myriad of lessons that have helped make me a better disciple of Christ. And two of my strongest partners in the gospel? My parents.

For those who long for marriage, allow me to remind you that first and foremost, a spouse should be your partner in the gospel. Tony Evans[37] suggests the term "spirit mate" instead of soul mate, thus emphasizing the importance of being equally yoked (2 Cor. 6:14) and the priority of supporting one another's spiritual health in the most intimate of relationships.

That type of support and encouragement in our spiritual walk can and should come through all of the other one-another relationships we form in the body of Christ. However, **our spiritual well-being is not dependent on anyone else.**

Is it a reasonable expectation that the church will meet my needs as a single or single-again woman?

There is no perfect nor universal answer to that question. If we are honest, it is more complicated than a simple yes or no. Yet, God does have a place and a purpose for the one-another relationships in the church, especially for those who are exceptions to the expectations. Elizabeth explains this term,

> Because most of the places that I have lived, I have not lived within a close proximity of my biological family. So, for that reason, church family has been even more significant. And we live in a world where

---

[37] Tony Evans, *Living Single*. (Chicago, IL: Moody Publishers, 2013)

that is the norm rather than the exception—you're typically not close by physical family. So as a church family, we need to be more aware of those individuals who are exceptions... and I don't mean that in an ugly way, but exceptions to the expectations. And find ways to be inclusive. That's not just in groups or small groups or Bible classes. It also comes in the form of the language that we use in public venues.

"The Language We Use" will be discussed in Chapter 25, but in the meantime, it is important for us to note that many of the exceptions to the expected norm are those who already feel that they have endured trials of many kinds. Many single and single-again women feel, like Hananiah, Mishael, and Azariah, that they have been through the fire, grateful that God has saved them. Whether a challenging marriage, a difficult breakup, or the persecution of living a pure life as a single woman... We each have our stories.

Throughout the pages of those stories, expectations have played their respective roles, whether expressed or implied. It is what we do with those expectations that is most significant. Do we become encaged by them, idolizing them and making them a "counterfeit god," as Timothy Keller proposes?

> ...we know a good thing has become a counterfeit god when its demands on you exceed proper boundaries. Making an idol out of work may mean that you work until you ruin your health, or you break the laws in order to get ahead. Making an idol out of love may mean allowing the love to exploit and abuse you, or it may cause terrible blindness to the pathologies in the relationship. An idolatrous attachment can lead you to break any promise, rationalize any indiscretion, or betray any other allegiance, in order to hold on to it. It may drive you to violate all good and proper boundaries. To practice idolatry is to be a slave.[38]

Idolatrous expectations keep us trapped in the CAJE. We feel that until our expectations are met, until someone else or some *thing* meets

---

[38] Timothy Keller, *Counterfeit Gods.* (Penguin Group, 2009), 23-24.

our expectations, we cannot break free. And since Satan longs to keep us encaged, expectations can be especially tricky.

Yet for good or for ill, we all have them. **When dreams become guidelines, the expectations are idolatrous.**

After we recognize these unhealthy expectations, we have to let them go. You may feel a sense of separation anxiety in releasing a dream, a hope, or a wish. Even the thought of letting it go can create a panicky feeling.

As a very visual learner, God granted me a special insight while meditating on 1 Peter 5:7 one night. *"Casting all your anxieties on him, because he cares for you."* (ESV)

Have you ever gone fishing? I grew up fishing with the family at the pond on grandpa's farm. Even though our little arms could barely cast a line, we knew that we had to cast the line or throw the baited hook out into the middle of the pond if we were going to have any hope of catching a fish for dinner. Sometimes we would ask for help with the casting (and of course with baiting the hook).

That night in 1 Peter 5:7, I realized several things.

1. I had never truly released to God my cares, my worries, my burdens, my expectations—whatever it was I was holding on to. Instead, I would explain them in great detail through prayer, providing God with all of the instructions He needed to meet my expectations with whatever situation I laid out before Him, and then promptly took them back into my own hands.

2. If I were to cast all my anxieties or circumstances on God, I had to picture myself going before God in His throne room, throwing whatever stuff at Him, and then running out of the throne room before I would pick it back up again.

3. When I truly let go of my expectations and my perceived control of the situation, I felt a tremendous burden lifted off of my shoulders. A literal weight was taken from me and I was free.

4. Yet I didn't quite know how to fly free and leave things in God's hands. I fell back into the trap of my own expectations and had to repeat the process day after day, night after night, until it became easier to trust God.

The more tightly we hold onto our expectations and the difficulty we have with letting them go are strong indicators of the hold they have on us. We may not realize how encaged we have become in the snare of their trap. And, ladies, if you also feel a sense of loss as you let go of your expectations, know that it is a normal part of the process. As we will discuss in Chapter 19, Acknowledge the Disappointment, the concept of mourning expectations is common and not without its specific challenges.

Our head may know these things, but our hearts hurt to hear them. **Anything—expectation or desire, person or image—that becomes more important to us than God, or that we look to for provision that only God can give, is an idol.** Allow me to repeat that: An idol is any expectation or desire, any person or anything that becomes more important to us than God, or that we look to for provision only God can give. Keller continues,

> It is not just those without spouses who need to see that God is our ultimate spouse, but those with spouses as well. They need this in order to save their marriage from the crushing weight of their divine expectations. If you marry someone expecting them to be like a god, it is only inevitable that they will disappoint you. It's not that you should try to love your spouse less, but rather that you should know and love God more.[39]

God's love for us knows no limits. Our love for Him should know no bounds. As Brandi has discovered,

> I've learned so much about God and how He meets us and interacts with us in singleness. Namely, I've grown in learning that

---

[39] Timothy Keller, *Counterfeit Gods*. (Penguin Group, 2009), 44-45.

expectations (met or not) absolutely cannot be my litmus test for God's love for me, investment in me, and involvement in my life.

One thing we can ALWAYS expect from God is His sacrificial, unconditional love. Keller eloquently describes our relationship with God.

> ...the God of the Bible is the one who comes down into this world to accomplish a salvation and give us a grace we could never attain ourselves. He loves the unwanted, the weak and unloved [like Leah]. He is not just a king and we are the subjects; he is not just a shepherd and we are the sheep. He is a husband and we are his spouse. He is ravished with us—even those of us whom no one else notices.[40]

His perfect love that drives out fear (1 John 4:18) transforms us because He is love (1 John 4:8). The radiant bride on her wedding day is glowing because she is filled with love and reflects the love she sees that her bridegroom has for her. **Ladies, God is our perfect bridegroom.** And we can love because He first loved us (1 John 4:19).

In the final chapter of this section, we will discover how God's perfect love sets us free from the CAJE traps and invites others into that same freedom of living out our one single reason.

---

[40] Timothy Keller, *Counterfeit Gods.* (Penguin Group, 2009), 44

CHAPTER 18

The CAJE Solution: Love

...because God is love. ⁹In this the love of God was made manifest among us, that God sent his only Son into the world, so that we might live through him.
(1 John 4:8b-9, ESV)

The best way to avoid the traps and to get out of them when we feel stuck: Love!

We started this section in 1 Corinthians 12, but left the final statement of that chapter hanging without transitioning to the very next chapter...

³¹Now eagerly desire the greater gifts.
And yet I will show you the most excellent way.

13 If I speak in the tongues of men or of angels, but do not have love, I am only a resounding gong or a clanging cymbal. ²If I have the gift of prophecy and can fathom all mysteries and all knowledge, and if I have a faith that can move mountains, but do not have love, I am nothing. ³If I give all I possess to the poor and give over my body to hardship that I may boast, but do not have love, I gain nothing.

⁴Love is patient, love is kind. It does not envy, it does not boast, it is not proud. ⁵It does not dishonor others, it is not self-seeking, it is not easily angered, it keeps no record of wrongs. ⁶Love does not delight in evil but rejoices with the truth. [7] It always protects, always trusts, always hopes, always perseveres.

[8] Love never fails. But where there are prophecies, they will cease; where there are tongues, they will be stilled; where there is knowledge, it will pass away. [9] For we know in part and we prophesy in part, [10] but when completeness comes, what is in part disappears. [11] When I was a child, I talked like a child, I thought like a child, I reasoned like a child. When I became a man, I put the ways of childhood behind me. [12] For now we see only a reflection as in a mirror; then we shall see face to face. Now I know in part; then I shall know fully, even as I am fully known.

[13] And now these three remain: faith, hope and love. But the greatest of these is love. (1 Cor. 12:31—13:13, NIV)

1 Corinthians 13 is often quoted in wedding ceremonies, but the context of this description of love directly follows the one-another relationships as distinct members of the body of Christ described in the preceding chapter (1 Cor. 12).

Love does not envy nor fall into the trap of **comparison**.

Love does not boast nor is it proud enough to **assume** it knows the other person's story.

Love keeps no record of wrongs, nor does it encage someone in a box of **judgement**.

Love always trusts, always hopes, always perseveres as God transforms our **expectations** and the desires of our heart.

Our one single reason is also our one single solution: love. 1 John 4:7-12 affirms this breaking through of our CAJEs.

[7] Dear friends, let us love one another, for love comes from God. Everyone who loves has been born of God and knows God. [8] Whoever does not love does not know God, because God is love. [9] This is how God showed his love among us: He sent his one and only Son into the world that we might live through him. [10] This is love: not that we loved God, but that he loved us and sent his

Son as an atoning sacrifice for our sins. ¹¹ Dear friends, since God so loved us, we also ought to love one another. ¹² No one has ever seen God; but if we love one another, God lives in us and his love is made complete in us.

(1 John 4:7-12, NIV)

God's love truly puts everything else in perspective. When we seek first His Kingdom and His righteousness (Matt. 6:33), the CAJE traps become more obvious in contrast to the loving freedom He offers through His perfect love.

God's Love Redefines Us

Always feeling **compared** to her beautiful sister Rachel, Leah became the matriarch of Christ's lineage. After recognizing that God's love mattered more than her husband's, the unloved of the sister wives named her fourth son Judah, which means "praise the LORD" (Gen. 29:35). A newfound love for God transformed her CAJE into a lineage.

Leah, Loved and Remembered.

Many **assumed** Timothy was too young to lead. Yet his mentor reminded him, *"Don't let anyone look down on you because you are young, but set an example for the believers in speech, in conduct, in love, in faith and in purity"* (1 Tim. 4:12, NIV). In love! Did you catch that? Love is pivotal to breaking out of any CAJE assumptions and fulfilling the identity that God offers.

Timothy, Loved and Recognized.

We see the **judgement** of condemnation being passed on the woman caught in adultery in John 8. Caught in the act, the scribes and Pharisees brought her to Jesus to trap Him. However, Jesus reminded them that none of them were free from sin either.

¹⁰ Jesus stood up and said to her, "Woman, where are they? Has no one condemned you?" ¹¹ She said, "No one, Lord." And Jesus said, "Neither do I condemn you; go, and from now on sin no more." (John 8:10-11, ESV)

Freed from the CAJE, we won't keep her there anymore either. No longer the adulteress, her identity was made new.

Woman, Loved and Repentant.

He was feared by the Christians, then blinded by the Lord, in order that he might see (Acts 9). Saul broke free from CAJEs in which he had originally prided himself (Phil. 3:4-11). No one **expected** Saul, the persecutor of the church, to become Paul, the church planter, but God saw the potential of a new identity in Him.

Paul, Loved and Repurposed.

God's love was the first step and the catalyst for each of these individuals' lives and identities being redefined. Yet take a moment and reflect on how many others were impacted by their freedom from the CAJE. I love to see the ripple effect of God's love when we allow it to work in and through us.

How have you seen the effects of God's love?

If you are longing to be free and to be transformed, let's take a moment to remember that this did not happen overnight for Leah, Timothy, the woman, nor Paul.

God's unwavering, deep love was needed over the time it took Leah to have three boys. Intentional mentoring, even after having grown up in the church, demonstrated the consistent love and direction Timothy needed. The forgiven woman was filled with love, shown through Christ's grace and mercy. He invited her into the work it would take her to live out love instead of the false identity of the embarrassing moment in front of the crowd of men. And Paul, one of our champion singles, took three years of preparation in the desert (Gal. 1:15-18), after having been shone down on and shown God's love.

When we allow ourselves to be transformed by True Love, we are freed from the CAJEs and our identities as God's beloved are formed.

God invites each of us into an identity that He redefines and through which we can glorify His name. Sydney reminds us of this with one of her own observations.

> I think it's important to recognize that although [marriage and family] are outlets in which you can definitely glorify God, there are so many things beyond that in which we have the ability to glorify God and we shouldn't try to find identity in those things.

Kari A., a divorcee and single mom, realized that much of her identity was wrapped up in her husband.

> I've had to find my new identity, and that can be a little tricky because you're like, at one point I had all these big dreams and aspirations as a kid. Now I don't even remember what they were. I'm sure I'm not doing them.

Recalling various memories during her interview, Kari recognized that the early **expectations** she had for her life were not met. She had **assumed** that her life would be great since she did marry a Christian man. Yet **comparing** her life to those of others became more entrapping because it highlighted how she felt that she had fallen short. Longing for liberty, she looked to God for His freedom from harsh **judgement**. She gave thanks for God's provision during that very difficult time of adjusting to being single again. And now, she can speak about those things with a confidence in God's love for her, for her children, and even His love for her ex-husband who has not yet come to repentance.

When discussing unmet expectations with others, it can be easy to get defensive. **Even in defending a good thing, we may lose sight of whether it is a God thing.** Sydney spoke to this point, as well.

> The belief that happiness can only be found in relationships, or in a marriage/ family is so toxic. Relationships are good things, marriage can be a good thing, and obviously a family can be a good thing, but a good thing does not necessarily mean it's a God thing.

Special thanks to all the women whose voices we have heard in this section on Avoiding the CAJE Traps. It is not easy to be open and honest in areas that are already vulnerable. However, once we have been freed, we long to welcome others into God's perfect love, as described in 1 Corinthians 13 and 1 John 4.

What is your identity, framed by God's love instead of through the bars of the CAJE traps?

SECTION IV

Table Talk

E ach of the traps has its own tenacity and agenda for keeping us encaged. Comparisons steal our contentment. Assumptions make us skeptical, doubtful, and negative. The snowball effect of real or perceived judgements twists us into a tailspin of destruction with our own whirling thoughts. And expectations, especially those that are unmet, can keep us feeling isolated and marginalized.

Yuck! Free me from the CAJE! As we take captive every thought and make it obedient to Christ (2 Cor. 10:5), may we dwell richly and deeply in His love that frees us from the darkness (John 3:16-21).

Talk with God (Personal Reflection Questions)

Any initial takeaways or thoughts from this section?

Which of the four traps is the greatest challenge for you personally? Comparisons, Assumptions, Judgements, or Expectations

Name at least three false assumptions you personally have made about others—single women, women who are single again for any reason, married couples, or about other Christians.

Name a specific expectation that has not been fulfilled. (We will revisit this in Chapter 19, Acknowledge the Disappointment.)

What has helped you successfully get out of a CAJE trap in the past?

Talk with an Iron Rose Sister

 In looking at the **Common Threads** for this Section, I invite you to be very intentional about how they apply to the CAJE traps in your lives.

 An area in which you want to grow or bloom

 A thorn you'd like to remove (a CAJE trap that seems to have a hold on you)

An area in which you'd like to dig deeper or need someone to hold you accountable

Remember, the Common Threads are shared with at least one other person in order that we can serve as iron sharpening iron (Prov. 27:17), encouraging each other to be as beautiful as a rose, in spite of a few thorns.

Table Talk with Others (one-on-one or group discussion)

The CAJE traps in the 1 Corinthians 12 description of the body of Christ are only *one* way in which we see the CAJE traps in the Bible illustrated. What are other examples of Comparison, Assumption, Judgement, and Expectation traps?

What are your thoughts about the definition of each of the CAJE traps? Are there any you would add to the list or remove?

How have you seen love break down the walls of the CAJE traps?

Comparisons:

Assumptions:

Judgements:

Expectations:

In addition to the conversation about God's love, how else, specifically, can we break down the CAJE traps in our own minds?

And now, how can we break down CAJE traps in the minds of others? Or can we?

Name a few additional false assumptions that are made about single or single again women. Don't include any names, but be specific about the way in which the assumption was false and how to reframe it with truth, spoken in love.

Name a few false assumptions single or single-again women have made about other church members. Don't include any names, but be specific about the way in which the assumption was false and how to reframe it with truth, spoken in love.

Would anyone like to share their "But even if God does not..." statement to which "to God be the glory" is your response (pg. 154)?

Describe your reaction to the contents of these chapters. Please explain where you are coming from. As you dialogue about this, be sure to listen, learn, and love one another, especially if there is something you agree with, disagree with, or would like to provide additional insight about from your own experience.

How have your insights or perceptions changed after discussing aspects of this section with someone else?

Walk the Talk

What is one single **Action Step** you can take or next-step conversation to have with others?

How can we help an Iron Rose Sister recognize the CAJE traps in her life? In pointing out these obstacles, don't forget to Offer a PEAR: Prayer, Encouragement, Activities, and Reminders of Truth!

Tips for Small Group Table Talk

Use 1 Corinthians 12 and 13 as the foundations for your discussion about the CAJE traps, especially if you are short on time.

This is the longest section in the book. It may be a good idea to plan ahead and split the conversation into two weeks (if you have time) or smaller groups (if you have space).

Section V

Responding APTLY

I am not saying this because I am in need, for I have learned
to be content whatever the circumstances. (Phil. 4:11, NIV)

We are faced with the challenge of responding to internal monologues, negative self-talk, Satan's lies, life-long expectations, and our unreliable emotions. The external factors complicate matters through comments made by others, relationship dynamics, family history, societal norms, and an implied or explicit pressure from others. These lists are not exhaustive. **How we respond to these internal and external pressures regarding our singleness can lead to contentment or resentment.**

Triggers set off a visceral response while, at other times, the same trigger can be shrugged off like water on a duck's back. It is important to identify our vulnerable times, places, topics, and circumstances. This is part of protecting yourself, the P of responding APTLY, which we will study in this section.

Thank you for your tolerance of my multiple acronyms. I am a forgetful person and therefore employ memory strategies and other techniques for recalling what is important. Acronyms are one such tool.

In this section, we will learn about responding APTLY: Acknowledge the Disappointment, Protect Yourself/Pray, Thank God, Love Others, and Yearn for the Right Things.

Responding appropriately or APTLY leads to contentment and great gain (1 Tim. 6:6). We are not alone in the journey toward contentment. We rejoice in a tremendous blessing when we can "*...be* **content** *with what you have, because God has said, 'Never will I leave you; never will I forsake you'*" (Heb. 13:5, NIV). God has not abandoned us! **In addition to Himself, God has given us each other as encouragers who are at different points along the road of contentment.**

In Philippians 4, Paul states that he has learned to be content whatever the circumstances and that he has even learned the secret of being content in all situations (Phil. 4:11-12). It is in the context of his contentment that he expresses, *"I can do all things through [Christ] who strengthens me"* (Phil. 4:13, ESV).

The contentment Paul boasts was not an immediate gift from God like the Holy Spirit that we receive at baptism. Rather, he had *learned* to be content. Learning is a process. A baby doesn't learn to walk the first time she stands up. A talented musician still must learn to hone her craft. The chef learns new techniques on how to cook culinary masterpieces. **We learn to be content.** If you aren't feeling content right now, don't let Satan ensnare you with his lies. Instead, let's replace his lies with truth and journey together in the learning process of how to respond APTLY and how to learn to be content. The book of Philippians will guide our discussion in this section, so be sure to read the verses at the start of each chapter.

CHAPTER 19

Acknowledge the Disappointment

7 But whatever gain I had, I counted as loss for the sake of Christ. 8 Indeed, I count everything as loss because of the surpassing worth of knowing Christ

Jesus my Lord. For his sake I have suffered the loss of all things and count them as rubbish, in order that I may gain Christ. (Phil. 3:7-8, ESV)

I will never forget the feeling of relief when someone put my struggle into words. In an attempt to describe the pain following a broken engagement, I compared it to my arm being cut off and blood gushing from my shoulder. My frustration grew as the first counselor seemed to ignore the gushing blood in preference to a focus on my pinky toe and what had happened in my childhood.

"Can we please address what is screaming first?" I asked, as my voice restrained its own scream. "I am not unwilling to dig up whatever from my childhood, but I can't even think about that without first putting a tourniquet on my arm to stop the bleeding!"

Even after using the analogy of the loss of a limb to describe my pain, I did not connect my circumstances with the grief one goes through after a loss.

For years, I had taught on the concept of mourning expectations. Somewhere in the intellectual part of my brain, I knew that grief was not exclusively associated with the death of a loved one, but rather applied to any sort of loss—the loss of a dream, a desire, a friendship...

However, the emotional part of my brain couldn't process that truth. When it came to my own situation, I was too close to see what was happening. My pain had blinded me to the need to process my grief. When a licensed counselor at church asked a coworker how I was doing, his response was, "Not well. It would be good for you to talk with her."

"What you need is grief counseling."

In expressing frustration over the first counselor that I was seeing, the second licensed counselor, and my friend, patiently listened and then simply said, "What you need is grief counseling."

A light bulb turned on. An epiphany was reached. Previously unwilling to start all over with a new counselor, I realized that when my feelings were defined and steps toward healing were offered, I was more than willing to take another first step and start over.

Over the course of the next several weeks and even months, I began to process my grief and mourn the expectations. The process of mourning expectations was one I was previously familiar with, but not to the degree that I faced with a broken engagement two weeks before my 35th birthday. Waves of grief washed over me as we peeled back the layers of the various things I was mourning.

As with any type of grief, everyone faces it differently and may go through it more quickly or slowly, sporadically or methodically. The theory of grief, originally presented by Elizabeth Kubler-Ross, is not a linear model. Different people will spend differing lengths of time in each stage and may revisit a stage after having already faced it initially. The **five stages of grief—denial, anger, bargaining, depression, and acceptance**—are not always processed in this sequence, but this is the commonly accepted order of the phases.

Denial. After the ending of the relationship, I was in shock. I couldn't verbalize what had happened because it would have made it more real. Confronted with the task of letting everyone know that the wedding that was to take place in two and a half months was no longer happening, denial was not a stage I could stay in for very long, but was where I landed initially. I couldn't believe this was happening to me.

The **anger** part of grief was harder for me because I couldn't let myself be angry with someone I continued to highly respect. I was not angry that his free will had been exercised and expressed. But anger and frustration characterized much of my speech and actions, usually directed at others, even sometimes at God, until I could process my anger in a healthy way. **For me, with anger, I had to allow myself to go there so that I could leave there.** I knew I didn't want to be known as an angry person, but expressing anger, for example through a letter you never mail, is a good way to not sin in your anger. God does not command us to never be angry. Jesus was angry. But He never sinned in His anger. Job expressed his anger to God through questions and various expressions of his pain. Yet Job did not curse God nor did God rebuke him for his anger. Rather God demonstrated His sovereignty and affirmed the fact that He had never left nor forsaken Job. At the end of the book, Job reaffirms his trust in God's love and His ultimate plan.

> *42 Then Job answered the Lord and said:*
> *2 'I know that you can do all things,*
> *and that no purpose of yours can be thwarted.*
> *3 'Who is this that hides counsel without knowledge?'*
> *Therefore I have uttered what I did not understand,*
> *things too wonderful for me, which I did not know.* (Job 42:1-3, ESV)

Once I allowed myself to be angry at my ex and the ways in which he had hurt me and broken promises, **I learned how to be angry about unmet expectations and give all of those feelings over to God.** The emotions were not sinful, as I originally believed. Rather I learned from Jesus' example as a human being who walked this earth how to express healthy emotions in a holy way.

Statements like "What if..." "If only..." characterize the **bargaining** stage of grief. Feelings of guilt, remorse, and anxiety, coupled with the sadness may not sound like part of the bargaining phase. Attempting to regain a sense of control, we play back scenes and decisions as a way of analyzing how we could possibly end up with a different outcome.

During the bargaining stage, we can learn from our mistakes and gain wisdom for the future, or we can beat ourselves up for the million and one things we think we did wrong. Which sounds more promising and healthier? Regrets can send us back into denial or can propel us into the depression stage.

Depression, which for me was coupled with crippling anxiety, became my lonely companion for many months, even years. Denial had long been abandoned and anger was a stage I would briefly and occasionally revisit, but when depression settled in, I felt like a shell of my former self.

But God... I love that phrase! But God, in the midst of deep depression, brought a phoenix out of the ashes and inspired me with the name, purpose, logo, and vision of Iron Rose Sister Ministries. Less than one year after the broken engagement, still processing my grief and acknowledging my disappointment, the first small group Bible study book was published and hundreds of women were already being equipped to connect to God and one another more deeply through the blog, conferences, and the first book, *Human AND Holy.*

Not everyone has such a large-scale tangible testimony of how God can redeem circumstances that started out as the mourning of an expectation, but I encourage you to remember that we serve a God...

> [20]*...who is able to do far more abundantly than all that we ask or think,*
> *according to the power at work within us,* [21]*to him be glory*
> *in the church and in Christ Jesus throughout all generations,*
> *forever and ever. Amen. (Eph. 3:20-21, ESV)*

The same power that raised Jesus from the dead is the resurrection power that can help us acknowledge the disappointment, put it in His capable hands, and trust that He can transform the desires of our heart in seemingly miraculous ways.

For the women who are single-again reading this book, I can imagine that you identify with at least some ways in which I processed the grief after my broken engagement. Please allow me to say how sorry I am for your loss, not just of a husband, but of the dreams that you had for your future. I see you. Your pain is real. Your loss is valid. And I am sorry for the way in which others communicate an expectation that you must explain or justify—even helping them process a grief that is not primarily theirs to bear.

For the single women, never married, a breakup can feel equally devastating. A milestone birthday can feel like the pronouncement of death on your dreams. Perimenopause hormones can feel like nails in the coffin of unmet expectations. I am sorry. I see you. Your pain is real. Your loss is valid. I am sorry that others may not understand the ways in which you may be mourning expectations, even while you are rejoicing with others whose dreams are being fulfilled through weddings, new babies, or even someday, grandchildren.

No two people's stories are exactly the same, but the commonalities are there. **The need for Christian fellowship and support as we acknowledge the disappointment and mourn the expectations is real.** Let's live out love through the highs and lows, the contentment, and the disappointment.

Acceptance is the final stage of grief. We have learned to be content, trusting in God and His ability to make all things work out for good (Rom. 8:28).

Please remember the encaging trap of comparison and let's not climb into that CAJE swapping one-upmanship stories to see who got to contentment faster or whose pain is worse. No! Pain is pain. Loss is loss. And the placating statements of others that minimize our grief are unwelcome. We each have different expectations and acknowledge the disappointment of their loss uniquely.

Alison never desired to get married, but rather has chosen to foster 11 children and adopted one with special needs. The expectations she had to mourn were not about marriage specifically, but were other dreams she had to let go of.

> I've kind of had to let go of a lot of the dreams, the typical dreams that people dream about. Like, I'm going to do this on my honeymoon, or I'm going to do this. And I've just kind of learned to... I'm going to live my life now and not think about the "what ifs," and really focus on what's now and what's present. **I've learned to be very content in what God has given me and let go of the other expected things that you think, "Most people get to do that."** And that's ok because I get to do other things. You know, there's times I'll go home at night and be

like, "Man, it would be really nice to have someone to share your day with." Most people have that. No, I don't have that, but I have really great friends, and when I want to call them and talk to them about it, they're available to me and we can have a great time. And I get all that time when [my daughter] is asleep until I go to bed on my own to do whatever I want to do. You know, there's tradeoffs, so you just have to remember the tradeoffs. I feel like God has shown me that, to be contented and to be ok with a simple life.

What expectations are you holding onto? (Feel free to refer to your answer on page 167.)

Is there a time in which you have experienced the five stages of grief, acknowledging the loss and mourning the expectations? If you are going through a time like that right now, please know that you are not alone. You are not going crazy; you're grieving.

How do we respond when we know someone is facing feelings of loss or is mourning expectations? How can we support each other?

For the first week or so after the breakup, three friends (and later my parents) tag-teamed to ensure that I was not ever alone. They were that radical human presence that I desperately needed. That first morning, my friend brought her makeup over to my house to get ready there after dropping the kids off at school. Her offer to make me breakfast got me out of bed to fix my own. That evening, another friend brought her crochet and we watched TV from the two ends of my couch, not saying much more than a dozen words between us. Like Job's friends (before they opened their mouths), they simply sat with me and reminded me that I wasn't alone.

If we are the ones feeling the loss, we can acknowledge the disappointment and allow the grief to run its course. If we recognize someone else who is mourning expectations, radical human presence is the first step. Then, refer back to how we can offer a PEAR in Section II (Prayer, Encouragement, Activities, and Reminders of Truth).

The first part of responding APTLY is to Acknowledge the Disappointment and not ignore it. If we merely sweep it under the rug, rest assured the growing lump under the rug will trip you up in the future. God's love for you and His desire for you to have the best life He longs to give you is reason enough to engage with Him in the process of dealing with your expectations.

If we are having trouble giving our expectations over to God, we can ask for help to cast them (1 Peter 5:7). In Chapter 17, I shared how I entered God's throne room and learned to throw my cares on Him and run back out of the throne room before I could pick them back up. A prayer partner, Christian sister, or Iron Rose Sister are excellent candidates for helping us not have to enter the throne room alone. Someone who is cheering us on or quietly supporting us from the sidelines helps us feel less lonely when we take the step of casting.

Another great way to define the expectations we are mourning or the disappointments we are facing is with a Christian counselor. One single mom explained,

> I had grieved my marriage long before the divorce. But after the divorce, I realized how many other expectations I had held onto that I then had to grieve. I found an awesome Christian counselor who helped me walk through that and I am still processing how to grieve all of it. The grief hit me harder and in ways I didn't anticipate because of what my expectations had been for my life and how my life was ending up. Now I'm just being open to wherever God takes me. He has changed my expectations.

Love for God permits us to give our expectations over to Him and trust Him as He invites us to a place of contentment. Listen to how God has helped Erica transform some of her fears into contentment.

> I once thought that I would feel so alone and that I was scared to die alone without having a companion...but truthfully that is never a

guarantee either. I have sat with a few older women who had been married with families, and their husbands had previously passed. In many ways they were still facing all of the same fears that I thought that I would face in remaining single. **Through this, I have learned that happiness is found through the contentment of being what God has called you to be during your present state, and to seek His will joyfully with the aroma of Christ.**

Erica learned contentment through expressing her fears, listening to others, and finding joy.

Mixed Emotions

We are uncomfortable with conflicting emotions. Are you happy or sad? Yes. Are you confused or confident? Yes. Yet God meets us in the emotional storm and is not afraid of the tumultuous and potentially conflicting sentiments. When we take our joys and our sorrows to Him, He leads us to contentment, re-centers our focus, and leads us to respond in a healthy way—an invaluable blessing when the emotions threaten to consume us and dictate our response.

We all face singleness differently and we react differently to the emotions that come with our singleness. As we invite each other to have a seat at the table, we are creating a safe place to openly express the myriad of feelings. For example, this thirty-year old single woman said,

> I don't like when married people say that singleness is a gift and if I'm upset it's because I'm jealous. It's true I am jealous, but I'm also lonely, depressed, bored, pointless, empty, worthless, experiencing grief. It needs to be okay to say actually I'm grieving the loss of the connection I hoped for.

Happy and sad; joyful yet longing; content and discontent; peace-filled yet angry... The vast array of mixed emotions is enough to make anyone's head spin. As Courtney M. put it,

One of the biggest challenges single women face is the dichotomy of being genuinely happy for your friends when they get engaged/ announce a pregnancy AND feeling intense jealousy/ sadness at the same time. No one talks about that.

A single woman is invited to be part of a wedding party. She is extremely excited for her friend and rejoices with the couple. Yet she also longs to be the bride someday, not merely the bridesmaid. While single women celebrate the new babies in the congregation and are often among those who volunteer in the children's ministry, there are many who long to hold their own children in their arms. Many of the surveyed women who expressed these unmet desires, also expressed a longing to do things "the right way" [41] **They are determined to find and marry a Christian man, then start a family together.**

Yet the clock is ticking; the field is narrowing. There may be more fish in the sea, but "I'm stuck in this pond where the only fish can best be described as piranhas!"

Mixed emotions are tricky. The children's movie *Inside Out*[42] did a fabulous job of illustrating that emotions are not an either/or, but rather a both/and. While we are acknowledging the disappointment and processing our grief, we can also feel intense joy in the opportunities God has given us as a single woman to serve. We count our blessings, "Thank God," and "Love Others" (the T and L of APTLY, which we will discuss later in this section), yet the sadness does not leave us.

For us women, the hormonal rollercoaster of life can leave us feeling like we are a slave to our feelings and reactions. Shifting hormones at certain times of the month can feel like vertigo has hit

---

[41] A smaller number of those surveyed expressed a desire to have children through solo adoption.

[42] *Inside Out*, directed by Pete Docter and Ronnie Del Carmen (2015; Disney Pixar).

our thoughts and emotions. Just give me a Rom-Com, some chocolates, and leave me alone for a week.

Just like Riley from *Inside Out* experienced, joy, sadness, anger, disgust, and fear coexist with other intense emotions that we sometimes cannot describe with a single word. We tend to avoid the seemingly negative emotions because of the deterrent they can be in other relationships, but that does not make them any less real, valid, or present. If we aren't careful, those emotions will overshadow any of the other things we feel or prefer to express. This is one of the many reasons it is important to Protect ourselves.

CHAPTER 20

Protect Yourself/Pray!

And the peace of God, which surpasses all understanding,
will guard your hearts and your minds in Christ Jesus. (Phil. 4:7, ESV)

The concept of protecting yourself in a conversation with single women, outside of a Christian circle, may include references to birth control options, condoms, sexually transmitted diseases, and possibly a cursory mention of abstinence.

As already mentioned in Chapter 12 about our longing for physical affection, God has a beautiful design for sex within the exclusive context of marriage, which is only one facet of the sacred union between a husband and wife. Like a fire that warms or provides light in its proper contexts, it can be destructive if it is removed from its proper place.

While we will address the dynamics of protecting ourselves from sexual temptation, to neglect protective strategies from Satan's other attacks on us as single women would be a naïve endeavor. We are in a spiritual battle and we must be armed and ready for the panoply of battlegrounds on which war is being waged for our souls. Prayer is the other expression of the P in APTLY and a vital facet of the spiritual armor described in Ephesians 6:10-18 (ESV).

¹⁰ Finally, be strong in the Lord and in the strength of his might. ¹¹ Put on the whole armor of God, that you may be able to stand against the schemes of the devil. ¹² For we do not wrestle against flesh and blood, but against the rulers, against the authorities, against the cosmic powers over this present darkness, against the spiritual forces of evil in the heavenly places. ¹³ Therefore take up the whole armor of God, that you may be able to withstand in the evil day, and having done all, to stand firm. ¹⁴ Stand therefore, having fastened on the belt of truth, and having put on the breastplate of righteousness, ¹⁵ and, as shoes for your feet, having put on the readiness given by the gospel of peace. ¹⁶ In all circumstances take up the shield of faith, with which you can extinguish all the flaming darts of the evil one; ¹⁷ and take the helmet of salvation, and the sword of the Spirit, which is the word of God, ¹⁸ praying at all times in the Spirit, with all prayer and supplication. To that end, keep alert with all perseverance, making supplication for all the saints.

Living in the world, but not being of the world has its challenges. Navigating those tests can be an exercise in spiritual discernment and a balancing act more difficult than walking a tightrope. However impossible it may seem, through His Word and His Spirit, God has given us the tools to better prepare ourselves for spiritual battle and come out victorious because we are on His team.

The contexts in which we must be prepared to protect ourselves are not always because of a direct attack. Well-intentioned individuals can say something that rattles us to our core. A passing comment undermines our contentment. A compromising situation crumbles our resolve, or a feeling of aloneness blinds us to our true needs.

One way I learned to protect myself was to be prepared with a witty response when someone's comments sent me into a discouraging spiral of negative thoughts.

"No ma'am, I'm not being too picky. I'm just clear on what I'm looking for in a Christian husband and I'm not prepared to settle."

"Yes, I am very happy for you and your new husband. And I appreciate your desire to set me up with <insert name>, but that is not something I am looking for right now. Thanks."

"You doubt that I'm single and lovin' it, mostly? I'm just being honest. Many of my married friends would say they're married and lovin' it... mostly. How about you?"

"Did you assume this was the life I have chosen?"

"Jesus was single. It worked for Him."

"Paul was single. He even said in 1st Corinthians 7 that we can do more in service to the Lord and His church by being single. Right?"

One more: "Yes, I'm married... to Christ and His church. And He's the best husband ever!

I have to be careful with my tone of voice or level of snippiness as I respond. If I am holding back resentment, judgement, or anger, it may be best to hold my tongue and not say any of the aforementioned quips—to protect myself from having to beg forgiveness.

Through relationship and genuine conversations, we can learn when and how to respond. **The most important relationship and genuine conversation that will guide my responses is the one with**

God through prayer. When I ask God to help protect me, I can set healthy boundaries instead of shutting myself off completely.[43]

After a few negative experiences with men, trust issues became a bigger challenge. Attempting to protect myself from further vulnerability, I had closed myself off completely. I thought I was guarding my heart (Prov. 4:23), but it turns out I was building a wall so thick and deep that it took God's chisel to break down the barriers I had built around myself. **Sometimes we have to protect ourselves from ourselves.**

If I am stepping on your toes, please hear me out. God invites you to embrace the love He offers. **The negative self-talk, the hours spent beating yourself up, the regrets in which you have wallowed—none of those things define how God sees you.** You may think that "nobody likes me, everybody hates me, I guess I'll eat some worms," but God flips the script and reminds you that His love is infinite, unconditional, and specifically meant for you, yes YOU!

A profound acceptance of the depth of God's love for me was transformative. Every time I build back the walls of self-protection, God steps in and showers me with His brick-shattering love and puts me back on track for the ways in which He is my Protector, my Defender, and my Guide in navigating when to be vulnerable and when to protect myself in order to stay within His will and His ways.

Learning from her mom's regrets and her own mistakes, Bethany has made protecting herself a high priority.

> For me, it's been more out of protecting myself because I've learned from past experiences how jumping into something too quickly can really mess things up, and you end up with someone you really shouldn't be with just because you're caught up in all the excitement.

---

[43] For more information about setting boundaries, check out Dr. Henry Cloud and Dr. John Townsend's book *Boundaries: When to Say Yes and how to Say No to Take Control of Your Life.*

Which is nice if you are first talking to somebody and you're kind of interested, you're like, ooh, this is exciting. And that feeling is nice, and I don't think there's anything wrong with having that feeling sometimes, but it's always important to remember not to let that decide I want to be with this person. That I'm going to get closer to them and more into it whether emotionally or physically in any kind of way. So, I learned from my past mistakes how to protect myself by going very slow, and I think it's preserved a lot of good friendships that way.

Many other women expressed through the survey responses and follow-up questions that **one of the greatest challenges for single women is to protect ourselves from sexual temptations and/or the temptation of rushing into marriage with the wrong guy.** This challenge is intensified by the fact that there are not many godly single men in our churches.[44] The temptation is great to compromise on the qualifications of a godly husband. Ladies, many who have settled have deeply regretted it. Conversely, women who married good Christian men later in life will affirm, "It's worth the wait."

Solomon, in Song of Songs, warns us about this temptation.

Daughters of Jerusalem, I charge you
by the gazelles and by the does of the field:
Do not arouse or awaken love until it so desires. (Songs 2:7, NIV)

Joseph fled while being seduced by Potiphar's wife (Gen.39). He had declined many times before and worked to avoid being alone with her. When we resist the devil, who wants to trip us up, we are promised that he will flee from us.

[7]Submit yourselves therefore to God. Resist the devil, and he will flee from you. [8]Draw near to God, and he will draw near to you. (James 4:7-8, ESV)

---

[44] An observation mentioned by women in the surveys and interviews, specifically a greater challenge for blacks and Hispanics.

When we draw near to God and humble ourselves before Him, He will protect us and guide us where we should go. Sometimes, it is more about where we shouldn't go than where we should go...

Avoiding and resisting temptation is not a challenge exclusive to situations in a sexual context. It can also be circumstances that tempt us mentally, emotionally, physically, or spiritually. We can be proactive by protecting ourselves from compromising circumstances, especially when we learn to identify areas or contexts in which we are more tempted. Here are a few examples of recommendations.

- You don't have to engage in the questions others ask about why you aren't married.
- When you are feeling especially vulnerable, avoid the Rom-Com movies.
- Remember the comparison trap that can encage us? Social media can send us spiraling into all four of the CAJE traps.
- You can make Galentine's plans instead of having a Valentine's pity party.

Based on your own struggles, what suggestions would you add to this list?

Naomi provided an example of how to protect herself and others when faced with a potentially complicated situation.

I take care to draw healthy boundaries with my guy friends, especially the ones who are married. So many women get themselves into trouble by sharing a level of emotional intimacy with men—intimacy those husbands should save for their wives. An example being, a guy I've been friends with for many years was going through a difficult time, his wife having just had a miscarriage, among other things. I knew he needed to talk about it, but that he probably wouldn't. I would have loved to let him pour his heart out to me and be there for him, but I knew it wouldn't be a good idea to invite that. So, I called his sister, who is also a good friend, explained my concern and my boundary, and asked her to check on him. She respected that I kept that boundary, was totally willing to call him, and he got the emotional support he needed.

Solomon said, "Drink water from your own cistern," and I want to respect marriage, even while I am single.

Naomi's discipline in this area helped protect others just as she is intentional about protecting herself. One of the things she is protecting herself from is the consequences of unwise decisions. We don't need an overactive imagination to picture what might have happened in Naomi's story if she hadn't responded in the way she did.

Sister, if you have found yourself in a situation in which you didn't protect yourself from the outset, it is never too late to stop and protect yourself now. God always provides a way out (1 Cor. 10:13) and grants us the opportunity to repent and return to Him.

Yes, we should protect ourselves from foolish decisions and from the consequences of bad ones. But God is bigger than those circumstances, as well. **God does not love you any less and He longs for you to come let Him lavish you with His love as the apple of His eye, the delight of His day, and the best ever-loving husband you will ever have!**

What a blessing! God truly loves us and longs for us to live out our one single reason in love for Him and love for others. One way in which we can do that is to have the awkward or uncomfortable conversations about what it means to protect ourselves. Women want to dialogue about this.

I always want advice from older women. I believe the best support a woman can have is from another woman. I want to know how to teach the gospel, how to avoid temptation, how to encourage others.

Even if you are one of the youngest people reading this book, there is someone younger than you who can learn from what God has taught you up to this point. God has instructed the older women to teach the younger women in Titus 2:3-5, but this opportunity for mentoring and teaching is not exclusive to marriage. We single women have a responsibility to live out love with our younger counterparts and to model what it means to fulfill our one single reason as beloved single daughters of the King.

CHAPTER 21

Thank God

³ I thank my God in all my remembrance of you, ⁴ always in every prayer of mine for you all making my prayer with joy, ⁵ because of your partnership in the gospel from the first day until now. (Phil. 1:3-5, ESV)

Count your blessings instead of focusing on what you don't have.

¹² Not that I have already obtained this or am already perfect, but I press on to make it my own, because Christ Jesus has made me his own. ¹³ Brothers, I do not consider that I have made it my own. But one thing I do: forgetting what lies behind and straining forward to what lies ahead, ¹⁴ I press on toward the goal for the prize of the upward call of God in Christ Jesus. ¹⁵ Let those of us who are mature think this way, and if in anything you think otherwise, God will reveal that also to you. ¹⁶ Only let us hold true to what we have attained. (Phil. 3:12-16, ESV)

Survey respondents were nearly unanimous in echoing Paul's sentiment in 1 Corinthians 7:34, thanking God for the opportunities they have to serve as single women, without the entanglements of a husband or family at home. The freedom, flexibility, and independence were each mentioned as facets of their singleness for which they are thankful—specifically as it afforded them more opportunities to serve others.

We can determine whether we see our singleness as a blessing or a source of complaint. It often depends on our perspective. Angela R., a single woman, never married, provides her perspective.

> I've had the opportunity to grow in ways that I don't think that I would have if I had married early. My experience as a single Christian woman has caused me to challenge a lot of ideas that I don't think I would have questioned otherwise. While painful, my difficulties in finding a place within church culture have made me more aware of and compassionate towards others who may be on the margins for different reasons.

Or the perspective of a single-again woman:

> I have been a single person for approx. 22 years. I had/have the loving support of longtime friends and my family and have not experienced the loss/isolation that I know can happen. I was not interested in marrying again and that left me free to discover strength I did not realize I had. God has blessed me greatly and I am truly thankful.

Giving thanks to God for His love for us and the opportunity to grow in our relationship with Him is invaluable. A widow in Texas shared,

> Although days can be lonely, you never are because God's got your back and He is with me always, so you are able to have a closer relationship with God as this is who you talk with daily.

What can you thank God for today?

We must ask ourselves if our singleness is a blessing or a curse, an opportunity, or a liability. Jordan chooses to see it as a gift.

> The freedom, time, and energy to devote to ministry, other people, and what God calls me to do in the moment. I consider my singleness as a gift - just like any other life situation - that can be used to glorify God.

A thankfulness journal can be an excellent practice toward an attitude of gratitude. When we focus on what we have instead of what we don't have, our gratefulness overshadows other longings.

Anna, a widow in the temple after only seven years of marriage, chose to live a life of gratefulness and service to God. Her words of thanksgiving were expressed as worshipful praise, fasting and praying. God honored Anna with the blessing of meeting the Christ child before the end of her life (Luke 2:37-38). Imagine her words of thanksgiving!

Songs and psalms of praise can be helpful when we don't have the words to express thanksgiving in the moment. Many of the psalms start with a frustration or a lament, but then end in words of praise. When we take things to God, no matter how we are feeling or what we are thinking, He is able to put things in perspective. In the same way the persistent widow sought justice before the judge in Luke 18, we know that when we go to God in prayer, we are presenting our requests to the one who has the power to do something about it. **God is not afraid of our emotions, our frustrations, even our anger.** He gave us those feelings and can guide us to know what to do with them.

Psalm 13 is a great example of a lament. Most laments have three facets: the complaint or crying out to God, asking for help, then responding in trust and praise.

> *13 How long, O Lord? Will you forget me forever?*
> *How long will you hide your face from me?*
> *² How long must I take counsel in my soul*

194 • ONE SINGLE REASON

> and have sorrow in my heart all the day?
> How long shall my enemy be exalted over me?
>
> ³Consider and answer me, O Lord my God;
> light up my eyes, lest I sleep the sleep of death,
> ⁴lest my enemy say, "I have prevailed over him,"
> lest my foes rejoice because I am shaken.
>
> ⁵But I have trusted in your steadfast love;
> my heart shall rejoice in your salvation.
> ⁶I will sing to the Lord, because he has dealt bountifully with me.
>
> (Ps. 13, ESV)

When we cry out to God, He is faithful to meet us where we are, walk with us through asking for help, and guide us into a response of trust, praise, and thankfulness. Even in the midst of our sorrow, our anger, our frustration—no matter what our mixed emotions—we can learn to be content.

When we present our requests to God, no matter our situation, we are called to do so with thanksgiving.

> ⁴*Rejoice in the Lord always. I will say it again: Rejoice!* ⁵*Let your gentleness be evident to all. The Lord is near.* ⁶*Do not be anxious about anything, but in every situation, by prayer and petition, **with thanksgiving**, present your requests to God.* ⁷*And the peace of God, which transcends all understanding, will guard your hearts and your minds in Christ Jesus.* (Phil. 4:4-7, NIV)

Paul reminds us that we can gratefully rejoice, no matter our circumstances—even from jail! Remember in the previous chapter when we discussed protecting ourselves? Paul suggests that God's peace will do that—guard our hearts and our minds in Christ Jesus—a byproduct of learning contentment.

As we learn to respond with thankfulness, we are led to contentment. When we count our blessings and adopt an attitude of gratitude, we are learning contentment. Throughout the book of Philippians, Paul highlights those for whom he is grateful (Phil. 1:3-5;

2:19-30). He specifically thanks the Philippians for their support as they shared in his troubles (Phil. 4:14-19).

Finally, I echo Paul's prayer in Philippians 1:9 as we look to the L of APTLY. *"And it is my prayer that your love may abound more and more, with knowledge and all discernment."* (ESV)

CHAPTER 22

Love Others

So if there is any encouragement in Christ, any comfort from love, any participation in the Spirit, any affection and sympathy, ²complete my joy by being of the same mind, having the same love, being in full accord and of one mind. ³Do nothing from selfish ambition or conceit, but in humility count others more significant than yourselves. ⁴Let each of you look not only to his own interests, but also to the interests of others. (Phil. 2:1-4, ESV)

Out of the abundance of God's love for us, we are blessed to serve as a vessel of His love to others. Do you doubt His love for you? We can trust that He, in His infinite love, is sovereign. No circumstance or situation is beyond His ability to love, to redeem, or to weave into the tapestry of His greater story. YOU are His one single reason for dying on the cross. He loves you that much.

What does it mean to you that YOU are the one single reason God sent His Son (John 3:16-17)? Do you believe this truth?

As a response to His love, our one single reason, our motivation and purpose behind everything is love... Or is it?

Years ago, a close friend and I were invited to speak at a Ladies' Day. When she was introduced, the presenter mentioned how much of a loving person my friend is. And during the prayer before she spoke, another sister thanked God for how much love my friend shows to everyone she meets.

I confess that I remember nothing about what I am confident was an excellent class, taught by my friend. Instead, I pridefully became focused on the fact that I didn't think anyone would describe me as "loving." A presenter would be much more likely to mention things I had done versus a description of my motivation for doing those things. And, at that point in my life, to be honest, I did more things, even in service to others, more for the recognition of others than out of love.

Convicted of my pride, for the following year, I prayed every day, "Lord, please help me be so filled with your love that I cannot help but live an outpouring of that love to others."

I would love to report that from that day forward, I never lost sight of my proper motivation. However, for that time, it did help me focus on what it meant to live out love and remain motivated by our one single reason.

When I stopped focusing on myself and how others saw me, God was able to fill me more fully and completely with His love. It was a constant temptation to put myself back as priority number one, but the emphasis on God's love permitted some of the selfish tendencies to dissipate. I was then better able to be used as an instrument in God's hand. It was no longer about me, but about Him and His people.

²⁸And one of the scribes came up and heard them disputing with one another, and seeing that he answered them well, asked him, "Which commandment is the most important of all?" ²⁹Jesus answered, "The most important is, 'Hear, O Israel: The Lord our God, the Lord is one. ³⁰And you shall love the Lord your God with all your heart and with all your soul and with all your mind and with all your strength.' ³¹The second is this: 'You shall love your neighbor as yourself.' There is no other commandment greater than these."
(Mark 12:28-31, ESV)

Through the church, we have a tremendous opportunity to learn how to live out love through one-another relationships and practice loving others. Be an aunt. Love a sister. Respect a brother. Care for a grandparent. **Every time we live out love in relationship, we model Christ and His love to others.**

A young single sister shared that one of the greatest blessings of being single is that she can serve God and others more readily.

> Not having to worry about anyone to take care of like a spouse so you can up and go if you need to. An example would be like babysit at a moment's notice, go sit in the hospital with someone without worrying about taking care of anyone back at home, etc.

We can pray that God will illuminate the occasions in which we can live out love to others. When we are longing for a spouse and for a family, we can hear all the one-another passages in Scripture as a way to highlight the void. Or we can follow Brandi's suggestion as she responded to the survey. Let's "break the stigma that the titles of wife and mother are the ultimate goal of women." All of the other one-another relationships in our lives are also important opportunities for us to live out love and fulfill the greatest command.

These are all things that our head knows, but our heart struggles to accept. Does the Bible speak about marriage? Absolutely. Does God provide instructions for husbands and wives? Yes, some.

However, the vast majority of all the relational passages in Scripture are talking about the relationships with brothers and

sisters in Christ, with enemies, friends, coworkers, bosses, and those who do not yet know Christ.

Lori learned better how to love God and love others after she became single-again. And she welcomes any opportunity to share God's love and faithfulness with others.

I became single as a 54-year-old widow. My husband of 33.5 years passed away Jan. 14, 2017. I grew up with him and he was my life. I have been a member at my local Church of Christ since 1984. I was a faithful attender and pew sitter but never really "knew" my brothers and sisters. I had no personal relationship with God. My husband's passing caused me to make a choice. I chose to grab on to God's hand and never let go. It's been a wild ride and God and I have had a great time. I am involved in [Let's Start Talking], women's ministry and small groups. My son came back into my life 2 months prior to my husband's passing. This was only possible by God. Our story has touched so many lives because it shows God's faithfulness. Being single has been good for me. I have learned boundaries and know what I truly want should I marry again. God has helped me see that not all godly people get married. It's okay to be single. Serving the Lord is easier, and my faith has grown exponentially. Being single has helped me learn how to be a true disciple of Christ.

I love sharing my testimony about being reunited with my son. I gave him up for adoption and God brought him back in my life after 35 years. It was a closed and sealed adoption. I never saw him or held him until we met Nov. 5, 2016, only 2 months prior to my husband's passing. God is so good and so faithful!

According to survey results, there is a direct correlation between how content a woman is in her singleness and how her relationships with other Christian women have been strengthened. An even stronger correlation exists between being content in our singleness and our relationship with God being strengthened.

We are back to our one single reason: love. Love is not possible without a recipient. If I say, "I love..." you are waiting for me to fill in the blank with the object of my love. My love for God and my relationship with God both grow as I learn to be content in my singleness. They go hand in hand. In addition, when my contentment in my singleness grows, my love for others and my relationships with others grow too, especially my relationships with Christian women.

Living out love is a crucial response if we are to arrive at a place of contentment. When we are filled with doubts, fears, or negative self-talk... When we are challenged by others or discouraged by their comments... When the accuser attacks and bombards us with lies... we can learn contentment when we respond with love.

One final encouragement for this chapter is to love through the eyes of a child.

> Upon arriving in our new home in Kentucky, my seven-year-old-son, Jason, decided to explore the neighborhood. He was back within the hour proclaiming that he had made some new friends.
>
> "Good. Are they boys or girls?" I asked.
>
> "One is a boy, and one is a girl," he replied.
>
> "That's great," I said. "How old are they?"
>
> "Mom," my son replied, "that would be very rude to ask."
>
> I was puzzled by his response, but about an hour later, Jason was back. "Mom!" he shouted through the screen door. "I found out how old my new friends are. The girl is sixty-five, and the boy is seventy."[45]

Who can you show love to today and how?

---

[45] Teri Leinbaugh in Edward K. Rowell and *Leadership*, editors. *1001 Quotes, Illustrations, and Humorous Stories for Preachers, Teachers, and Writers.* (Grand Rapids, Michigan: Baker Books. 2008), 352.

CHAPTER 23

Yearn for the Right Things

⁸ Finally, brothers, whatever is true, whatever is honorable, whatever is just, whatever is pure, whatever is lovely, whatever is commendable, if there is any excellence, if there is anything worthy of praise, think about these things. ⁹ What you have learned and received and heard and seen in me—practice these things, and the God of peace will be with you. (Phil. 4:8-9, ESV)

T he final way in which we can respond APTLY is to "Yearn for the Right Things." The more we focus on something, the more we want it. This is to our benefit and detriment.

Stephen R. Covey wrote one of the best-selling non-fiction business books in history, *7 Habits of Highly Effective People*. His second habit, "Begin with the end in mind," echoes God's teaching throughout the pages of the Bible (as seen in the following verses). As you read these passages of Scripture, ask yourself, "What is my goal?" "What is the end I have in mind?"

For as he thinks in his heart, so is he. (Prov. 23:7, NKJV)

¹⁰ And whatever my eyes desired I did not keep from them. I kept my heart from no pleasure, for my heart found pleasure in all my toil, and this was my reward for all my toil. ¹¹ Then I considered all that my hands had done and the toil I had expended in doing it, and behold, all was vanity and a striving after wind, and there was nothing to be gained under the sun. (Eccl. 2:10-11, ESV)

Matthew 6:33 and the admonition to seek first God's Kingdom and His righteousness come on the dovetails of this invitation to not worry.

²⁵ "Therefore I tell you, do not worry about your life, what you will eat or drink; or about your body, what you will wear. Is not life more than food, and the body more than clothes? ²⁶ Look at the birds of the air; they do not sow or reap or store away in barns, and yet your heavenly Father feeds them. Are you not much more valuable than they? ²⁷ Can any one of you by worrying add a single hour to your life?

*²⁸ "And why do you worry about clothes? See how the flowers of the field grow. They do not labor or spin. ²⁹ Yet I tell you that not even Solomon in all his splendor was dressed like one of these. ³⁰ If that is how God clothes the grass of the field, which is here today and tomorrow is thrown into the fire, will he not much more clothe you—you of little faith? ³¹ So do not worry, saying, 'What shall we eat?' or 'What shall we drink?' or 'What shall we wear?' ³² For the pagans run after all these things, and your heavenly Father knows that you need them. ³³ **But seek first his kingdom and his righteousness, and all these things will be given to you as well.** ³⁴ Therefore do not worry about tomorrow, for tomorrow will worry about itself. Each day has enough trouble of its own.* (Matt. 6:25-34, NIV)

"Each day has enough trouble of its own." I have been known to quote that word of caution from Jesus as a reminder to myself that I don't have to get everything done in one day. God's timing is best, and His ways are perfect. My stress level really is indicative of where my focus lies—and not just on the topic of singleness.

When we strive to find ways to serve, God provides. When we lift up our requests to Him, He is faithful to answer. It may just not be the answer we were hoping for, nor in the timing we would've preferred.

Do you sometimes wonder if one single reason is enough motivation to keep waiting? If that one single reason is a love for Christ and a desire to live out His divine plan for your good, then yes.

202 • ONE SINGLE REASON

That is reason enough. His love for you and His desire for your good is greater than any other love you can comprehend.

It is not wrong to want to be in a relationship, but if we desire that above all else, we have idolized it and removed God from His rightful place as top priority.

> Idolatry is not just a failure to obey God, it is a setting of the whole heart on something besides God. This cannot be remedied only by repenting that you have an idol, or using willpower to try to live differently. Turning from idols is not less than those two things, but it is also far more. "Setting the mind and heart on things above" where "your life is hid with Christ in God" (Col. 3:1-3) means appreciation, rejoicing, and resting in what Jesus has done for you. It entails joyful worship, a sense of God's reality in prayer. Jesus must become more beautiful to your imagination, more attractive to your heart, than your idol. That is what will replace your counterfeit gods. If you uproot the idol and fail to "plant" the love of Christ in its place, the idol will grow back.[46]

I must constantly ask myself, "Where is my focus? Where have I set my heart?" When I slip into asking questions like, "But will I ever get married?" or "How could this have happened to me?" my focus is off, and my idols are back.

I must yearn for the right things—place them at the forefront of my mind and in the center of my heart. A love for God and a love for others really is our one single reason. It truly puts everything in perspective and helps us recognize our blessings, learn contentment, and avoid the CAJE traps. Listen to how these three women have maintained their focus.

When asked about some of the greatest blessings as a single woman, Angela M. answered,

---

[46] Timothy Keller. *Counterfeit Gods*. (Penguin Group, 2009), 171-72.

Like 1 Corinthians 7 says, being able to focus more on ministry/serving others, more time with God. Becoming more independent and finding your own voice.

Angela R. mentioned a compliment a married friend shared about her time as a single woman.

From a friend who has been married over twenty years, and who I have always looked up to: "I really admire you single women, and all that you are able to do. I realize that I have never developed those parts of myself as I had a husband to lean on." It was so incredibly affirming to have a married person recognize that singleness could actually teach a person valuable things that they might not learn in marriage.

My friend Julie is a gifted singer. Since she is single, she has been able to use her gift of a beautiful voice to travel more freely, in a praise and worship group, encouraging others through song.

Each of these women has strived to keep her eyes fixed on Jesus, the head of the body and the perfecter of our faith.

12 Therefore, since we are surrounded by so great a cloud of witnesses, let us also lay aside every weight, and sin which clings so closely, and let us run with endurance the race that is set before us, 2 looking to Jesus, the founder and perfecter of our faith, who for the joy that was set before him endured the cross, despising the shame, and is seated at the right hand of the throne of God. (Heb. 12:1-2, ESV)

Our focus on Christ can waver when we get distracted or long for the wrong things. That is why it is important to cheer each other on from the great cloud of witnesses. Charissa suggests ways in which we can support single women.

[By allowing] women who have experienced times of singleness to tell their stories and give advice about how to trust God concerning the future. Also, less discussion of marriage relationships and more talk about the value of waiting and strengthening your relationship with Jesus is very encouraging.

Ladies, it is my prayer that through the pages of this book, you have been encouraged to know that you are not alone and that you have been cheered on to focus on the right things. Our one single reason has grown through our love for God, for one another, and for ourselves. We have learned to be more content. And I can't wait to see what else God does in your lives!

SECTION V

Table Talk

When we respond APTLY, we are filled with contentment. It can be difficult to always respond appropriately to others, especially when they push our buttons or touch on a sore subject. Our internal doubts and fears may be even more tough to respond to, but God has not left you nor forsaken you. He sees you and strengthens you, holding you in His right hand (Is. 41:10, 13).

Learning contentment is a worthwhile process. On our journey toward contentment, may we serve as silent human presence for those who are **acknowledging a disappointment** or mourning expectations. May we support one another in **prayer** as we **protect ourselves**. **Thanking God** becomes an easier practice when done with others. **Loving others** offers us the opportunity to keep our focus where it should be—**yearning for the right things** with our eyes fixed on Jesus.

Talk with God (Personal Reflection Questions)

Which are the easiest and hardest response for you and why?

Acknowledge the Disappointment

Protect Yourself/Pray

Thank God

Love Others

Yearn for the Right Things

Acknowledging the Disappointment and mourning expectations is not always event-based or a clearly defined moment. Rather, it can sneak up on you and present itself unexpectedly. Is there an expectation you are mourning currently?

Is there someone specific you want to invite to the table of this conversation in responding APTLY? It may be someone to whom you didn't respond appropriately before. It may be someone who is also striving to learn contentment. Whoever it is, I encourage you to reach out to them and offer them a seat at the table.

Talk with an Iron Rose Sister

In looking at the Common Threads for this Section, we have an opportunity to cheer one another on from the great cloud of witnesses.

The **Common Threads** are found in all Iron Rose Sister Ministries Small Group Bible Studies.[47]

Remember, the Common Threads are shared with at least one other person in order that we can serve as iron sharpening iron (Prov. 27:17), encouraging each other to be as beautiful as a rose, in spite of a few thorns.

 An area in which you want to grow or bloom

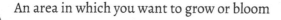 A thorn you'd like to remove (something that hinders you from responding APTLY)

An area in which you'd like to dig deeper or need someone to hold you accountable

This is a great opportunity to invite someone to hold you accountable in your responses and in your focus. You can also serve as buffers and reminders for each other when you are found in a challenging context.

Table Talk with Others (one-on-one or group discussion)

What verse(s) in Philippians most helps you respond APTLY?

---

[47] For more information about Iron Rose Sister Ministries, our small group Bible study materials, and other resources, including additional resources for facilitating this conversation with single women or church leaders, see Chapter 34, "About Iron Rose Sister Ministries," and visit our website, https://IronRoseSister.com/.

How has the topic of mourning expectations impacted you? What makes this conversation important to you?

Using Ephesians 6:10-18, describe the protection each facet of the armor of God provides single women.

Can you describe for me a context in which a single woman might need help from others to protect herself? How can others help avoid this from happening or help support and protect the single or single-again women in this situation?

Let's go around the room and each share something we can thank God for. I am grateful for each of your voices and perspectives in this conversation. I thank God for what I am learning through this dialogue.

What are some specific ways in which we can love others around this conversation table, in our local churches, and in our communities?

What does it mean to yearn for the right things in your current life situation? What is most helpful or encouraging to you in that effort?

Do you have any other comments or reactions to the contents of this section? Please don't forget to explain where you are coming from with your comments. As we dialogue about this, don't forget to listen, learn, and love.

How have your insights or perceptions changed after discussing aspects of this section with someone else?

Walk the Talk

What is one single **Action Step** you can take? Describe some next level conversations to have with others.

Have you thought about starting a thankfulness journal?

How will you live out love this week?

I encourage you to read the book of Philippians, four short chapters, as a reminder of each facet of Responding APTLY.

Tips for Small Group Small Talk

By this point in our Table Talk conversations, everyone is feeling more comfortable to share vulnerable aspects of their stories. Allow space for those who are grieving to talk, but it is okay to gently interrupt her with a prayer, affirm her, and offer to have a lengthier conversation in another setting.

Remind everyone (and yourself) that contentment is a process, which means every single person is in a different place on that journey.

Section VI

Congregational Strategies

¹⁵ For this reason, because I have heard of your faith in the Lord Jesus and your love toward all the saints, ¹⁶ I do not cease to give thanks for you, remembering you in my prayers, ¹⁷ that the God of our Lord Jesus Christ, the Father of glory, may give you the Spirit of wisdom and of revelation in the knowledge of him... ²² And he put all things under his feet and gave him as head over all things to the church, ²³ which is his body, the fullness of him who fills all in all. (Eph. 1:15-17, 22-23, ESV)

Before proceeding with our conversation of how to apply truths learned from and about single and single-again women in a congregational context, there are a few important things to remember:

- There is no one right answer that will apply in every congregation.
- Our primary goal is to learn how to live out our "one single reason": love.
- We seek to facilitate a conversation, not provide a perfect solution.

Many women provided similar suggestions and recommendations that I will synthesize by the popularity of their responses. Others offered concrete examples that merit their own mention. Finally, **the diversity of responses affirms that there is no one right answer nor one perfect solution to this issue.**

We are not here to air grievances, however in order to provide a contextual background for some of the suggestions, I may include specific quoted language of the single women who participated in the surveys and interviews.

Any resolution of the challenges faced by single and single-again women in the church brings us back to **the importance of relationship and communication.** Again, thank you for your willingness to engage in this conversation! Please invite others to dialogue with you about these topics. Learn from each other and hear each other's hearts. We all have amazing gifts and talents to offer the Lord's church. Our differences are a source of strength rather than an obstacle to allow Satan to exploit.

CHAPTER 24

Love is Our One Single Reason

[14] For this reason I bow my knees before the Father, [15] from whom every family in heaven and on earth is named, [16] that according to the riches of his glory he may grant you to be strengthened with power through his Spirit in your inner being, [17] so that Christ may dwell in your hearts through faith— that you, being rooted and grounded in love, [18] may have strength to comprehend with all the saints what is the breadth and length and height and depth, [19] and to know the love of Christ that surpasses knowledge, that you may be filled with all the fullness of God. (Eph. 3:14-19)

The book of Philippians guided much of our discussion in the previous section. This section takes us back to the book of Ephesians as Paul writes to a church that needs to be reminded of their unity in diversity. For this section, unless noted, verses are quoted from the NIV.

[15] Instead, speaking the truth in love, we will grow to become in every respect the mature body of him who is the head, that is, Christ. [16] From him the whole

body, joined and held together by every supporting ligament, grows and builds itself up in love, as each part does its work. (Eph. 4:15-16)

Speaking the truth in love... as each part does its work... We all have a job to do!

Love for God and love for others has been our central focus. Love of self as a single woman has also been a key element to our discussion thus far. Since love is our one single reason and motivation in these conversations, I feel it important that I overtly and directly say that I also love the church. **Most of the single women that I have surveyed and interviewed love the church, as well.**

However, we each approach the topic of singleness with a certain set of experiences within our respective church cultures that, more times than not, have served to dampen our passionate love for the church. We love her as the bride of Christ. We embrace her as the international body of Christ. Yet, within our respective congregational contexts, the local church's dynamics and culture, the challenges and insensitivities for single women are more evident and problematic.

Specifically, to my single sisters who are struggling because of past hurts that have happened in the church, I am sorry. I see your pain and want to hear your story. I pray that you can embrace the never-ending love God has for you and find your way back into regular communion and fellowship with His body, the church.

We are not in heaven yet, so we are going to have to deal with our own imperfections and those of others. Sometimes, that is tough! But it is worth it. Remember our one single reason? Love for God, love for others, love for ourselves as single women, AND love for the church. It's a package deal. If we speak ill of the church, we are speaking ill of the bride of Christ. Would we want anyone to speak ill of us in that way?

Ladies, please remember that even if we do not always feel welcomed or included, we also have unique gifts that have their place in the larger Kingdom context. We each have to do our part. And I pray that the things you have learned from the previous chapters can be applied to a variety of relationships, especially those in our household of faith.

"So then, as we have opportunity, let us do good to everyone, and especially to those who are of the household of faith" (Gal. 6:10, ESV).

Through our church family, we have the opportunity and the responsibility to be the best sister, aunt, daughter, niece, and granddaughter we can be. While it is vital for us to continue our service to others outside of a church context, please know that your local church needs you, as well. You have distinctive talents and passions that many of the younger women in the congregation need to see modeled. You are a vital part of the body that is missed if you are not there.

Single moms, you are modeling the priority of fellowship with other believers to your children. The extraordinary efforts you make on Sunday mornings to get everyone ready and out the door is worth it! We see you and the hard work you are doing, investing in the spiritual growth of your children. Thank you for modeling that priority to others!

CHAPTER 25

The Language We Use

²Be completely humble and gentle; be patient, bearing with one another in love. ³Make every effort to keep the unity of the Spirit through the bond of peace. ⁴There is one body and one Spirit, just as you were called to one hope when you were called; ⁵one Lord, one faith, one baptism; ⁶one God and Father of all, who is over all and through all and in all. (Eph. 4:2-6)

The most frequently mentioned response to what would make you feel more welcomed, invited, or supported by the church reflected the importance of the language we use—from the pulpit, in our bulletins, through our websites, and, of course, in our individual conversations.

A single sister, never married, shares the following insights about the language we use in our churches.

Any time you're working with a group of people, in order to be an inclusive group, the language used has to be mindful of that. The way that language typically in our faith tradition has spoken about men and women, has been husbands and wives, children, grandparents... Well, I am not a husband or a wife, technically I'm still a child, but that's not the function and the role that I live on a day-to-day basis. I am not a grandparent because I'm not a mother or a father. I am an aunt. I am a sister in Christ. I am also a woman or a daughter in Christ.

If we want to be more intentional about the language that we use, we need to be mindful of using language that the people who are hearing what's being said can see themselves in it. Because if we can't hear ourselves in the language, we don't feel included.

On Mother's Day, I appreciate the fact that in recent history, language has been adjusted to not just include mothers and grandmothers, but also to include mother-like figures. Because in my profession as an educator, there have definitely been students—while I've not been their biological mother—I've frequently played the role of a mother for them. And even to this day, will claim them as my non-biological children. And so, the inclusion of mother-like figures as a part of those messages that are shared on Mother's Day is a way to be more inclusive and more intentional with our language.

Single in Texas: "When speaking publicly (sermon, announcements, communion meditation, etc.) and giving examples, use examples of friendship, roommates, and siblings—not just marriage/spouse or relationships with your kids."

Jamie C.: I think the church should be more vocal about its single members, especially their older single members. Coming to college, I had never met someone over the age of 30 that wasn't married, so getting to meet people that chose that lifestyle was so encouraging to see. Not getting married is never the "worst case scenario" like I grew up thinking. In fact, there are infinitely more ways God can use single women to do His works. I think the church should have single women speak to high school and college-aged girls regularly to show them that they do not have to be married and they do not have to be ashamed about it.

Candace: "Church leaders should help foster an attitude of marriage being an 'if' not 'when.'"

Single woman in Oklahoma: Talk about being single! Talk about Scriptural teachings on being single. Talk about it as a valid life choice, an important state, an offering to God. Scripture says that it is GOOD to be single and serve God with undivided attention... but we don't act that way.

And talk about it to the kids—I came out of high school ready to get married, with a well-developed theology for being a wife and mother... but life looked like long-term singleness... I felt very alone and didn't have any kind of theology for understanding it. And there's just no reason for that.

The experiences shared by these women are not unique to them. Across the Americas I have spoken with, surveyed, and interviewed women who echo these sentiments. **They long to have singleness be a more normalized part of our conversations, sermons, and general language.** If around half of the population in the U.S. is single, how are we providing an environment that is inclusive of those single adults?

Is the language we use in church inclusive or exclusive for single women? What about for other individuals who may feel marginalized?

A church picnic is being planned... "We hope every family is able to be there!" or "We hope to see everyone there for the picnic!"

What to Say and
What Not to Say

Do not let any unwholesome talk come out of your mouths, but only what is helpful for building others up according to their needs, that it may benefit those who listen. (Eph. 4:29)

We all want to feel a sense of belonging. The book of Ephesians emphasizes our unity in Christ, and several verses affirm that what we say matters....

Section IV, Avoiding the CAJE Traps, provides a filter through which we can test our speech and conversation with single and single-again women. Here are a few questions to ask ourselves—not just in communication with single women: Am I inadvertently **comparing** this person to someone else or to my own **assumptions** or **expectations**? What false **assumptions** have I possibly formed about single or single-again women? Might my words be seen as a **judgement** of her current circumstances? Am I projecting my **expectations** on someone else?

In the words of many survey participants, here are some examples of the most discouraging or unsupportive language used. Names and any identifying characteristics have been intentionally omitted.

Negative comments heard by single women, never married:

- "You need to stop being so picky, just get married so you don't have to be lonely."
- "Why aren't you married?" I have never even been asked on a date. How do I even respond to that question? It makes me feel like I am somehow not enough.
- "You're still ok... it's when you hit 30 that it's getting too late."
- That I can only truly demonstrate God's love through marriage and child-raising. Everything else in my ministry among the poor pales in comparison.
- I always hate when people say, "Your time will come!" because I don't think that's promised.
- Spiritually, anything to do with a lack of recognition of my gifting because I am single. This fosters the idea that marriage is equated with maturity—both spiritual and emotional—which I find highly demeaning.

Negative comments heard by single-again women:

- If I was a Godly woman, my husband would not have left me. I've heard this by many people. I have not wanted to talk poorly about my husband, so I did not state that he was an adulterer. Even to the few that I tried to tell what was happening, I was called a liar.
- "Don't come and ask for help because you are single, it was your choice." (I had just gotten out of an abusive relationship!!!)
- I chose to have kids with the wrong person, and I have to deal with the consequences.

As you can see, whether intentionally or unintentionally, our words can be a stumbling block for our single sisters. *"Therefore let us stop passing judgment on one another. Instead, make up your mind not to put any stumbling block or obstacle in the way of a brother or sister"* (Rom. 14:13).

Now that we have seen what NOT to say, what are some of the things we should say?

Positive comments:

• Probably the most positive thing is when my marital status is not part of the conversation.

• On Mother's Day... after a comment about Happy Mother's Day/sorry, you're not a mom.... "Wait, yes you are, you're a mom to all those children out there at [workplace]."

• From a friend who has been married over twenty years, and who I have always looked up to: "I really admire you single women, and all that you are able to do. I realize that I have never developed those parts of myself as I had a husband to lean on." It was so incredibly affirming to have a married person recognize that singleness could actually teach a person valuable things that they might not learn in marriage.

• "Single people have exponentially more opportunities to engage God, relationships, community, and ministry than those who have familial obligations."

• "You can do what you would like to do without worrying about someone else. It is better to be single than in a bad relationship."

• "Your strength inspires and is noticed."

• "You are strong, and a great mom and your daughter is blessed to have you."

• "I am proud of what you have accomplished since your divorce."

Other positive comments were affirming of how single women have used their time, independence, and talents to God's glory.

The women surveyed indicated that they hear more positive comments from family than from society or the church. The most negative comments are heard from society (more often than from family or the church). In general, comments from the church are more evenly dispersed between positive and negative comments.

What does this mean for the purposes of our conversation? As affirmed through the short-answer and follow-up questions, positive comments carry more weight and are more appreciated when shared in the context of relationship.

According to a separate survey question, using a 4-point scale from highly encouraging (4) to highly discouraging (1), the women were asked how they were affected by remarks from different groups. Remarks from friends and family have the most encouraging effect as compared to all other groups' remarks (averaging 3.1 & 3.0, respectively). Remarks made in work or academic environments were a close third (2.9), following on the heels of family's encouraging impact. Local congregations provided context for the fourth and final group of encouraging remarks and their influence (2.6). Local and online communities did not have a significant number of encouraging remarks, nor did those comments have a significant effect on the women surveyed.

Our positive and encouraging remarks matter. They make a difference. And when made in the context of relationship, every single person feels less alone.

CHAPTER 27

Feeling Solo on Sundays

¹³And you also were included in Christ when you heard the message of truth, the gospel of your salvation. When you believed, you were marked in him with a seal, the promised Holy Spirit, ¹⁴who is a deposit guaranteeing our inheritance until the redemption of those who are God's possession—to the praise of his glory. (Eph. 1:13-14)

By focusing exclusively on the commonalities, we have developed separation of fellowships and division by demographics within the congregation (e.g., children's ministry, youth group, college class, young marrieds, etc.).

The widow, the visitor, the student... many more people than we realize are single on Sundays. Borrowing a term from one congregation in Colorado, "Single on Sunday," can refer to anyone who is not attending church with a spouse or significant other.

Some of the loneliest people I know are married and, in a church setting, identify more with single individuals than with those who are married. A friend of mine's husband has chronic health conditions that prevent him from attending church. Even though she is married, she is functionally single.

Another friend, divorced, feels a little less alone every other Sunday when her children are sitting with her, and she takes them to Bible class. However, the other weeks, less distracted by her children when they have visitation with her ex-husband, she sits alone.

Older single in Texas: "Invite singles to sit with you in church and to go out to eat with your family. I want to be included and be part of a family and not be considered a single. I would like to be in a class of mixed ages instead of classes divided by stages in life."

Single again in Arkansas: "If you know someone who's going through a divorce or has lost a spouse in one way or another, meeting them at their house and going to church with them for a while makes a world of difference. After 17 years of being with my husband, now I am so alone, and **the hardest time for me is walking through the doors of the church building**."

Ruth: "We have a class called SALT, Single Adults Living True. It is a mixture of men and women mainly from divorce, but we also have widows and widowers, women and men who have never married."

Young single: "Sunday can be one of the most lonely, isolating days for a Christian single. Invite them into your homes, ask them to sit with you at church."

Many elementary schools have a bench on the playground where children who are feeling alone can sit as a non-confrontational way to admit they are feeling lonely and are seeking a friend. One congregation has started a similar practice by designating an area in their auditorium as a "Solo on Sundays" section. Widows and single-again individuals have especially taken advantage of this practice. They will often create an impromptu invitation for anyone interested to go to lunch together after the services.

A church in Georgia has adopted the term Solo on Sundays to refer to a group of single women who meet after the services every other week to encourage each other through prayer and in-depth Bible study.

An additional note from a sister in Tennessee highlights an important point, the sentiment of which is echoed through other women's comments. **"We don't want to be 'singled' out. We want to be a part of the group.** There are other things you can have in common with people than just whether you are married or not."

Reactions were mixed whether these specific areas to sit or having a separate class were a positive or negative "singling out" of the singles. Remember: Dialogue with the single and single-again women in your congregation. They have a lot to give and will be your best advocates for helping the right things happen congregationally that bring other single women into deeper relationship with God and with others.

Finally, one concrete suggestion was made that I have seen adopted in various congregations successfully. Churches that have greeters can pay special attention to those who walk into the building by themselves on Sunday mornings. "Are you meeting someone this morning? If not, I would love to sit with you myself, or I know some ladies that would love to sit with you!" An invitation like this one offers a sincere welcome and less chance for someone to feel alone. If couples are serving as greeters, the wife can go ahead and sit down with the solo visitor, leaving the husband to continue greeting others. There are many ways in which we can be intentional about helping others feel welcomed as soon as they walk through the doors of our church buildings, and later our homes, and our lives. What a blessing to live out our one single reason in this impactful way!

Feeling Alienated through Sermons

In one of the congregations where I attended, a sermon series on intimacy was presented. The preacher did, in the first lesson of the series, speak to the fact that intimacy and trust issues can be issues in relationships outside of marriage. Yet the rest of the series focused almost exclusively on intimacy in the marriage relationship.

Determined to not let my emotions get the best of me, I prayed for strength.

However, another week or two into the series, one of the sermons triggered a PTSD-type panic attack. A request that the audience turn to their spouse and ask some of the "trust questions," presented in that sermon, served to highlight an aching hole that had been vacated by an ex—someone in whom I could no longer trust.

The primary question had to do with whether the spouse could trust their partner to make the other person his/her top priority. Ouch. Way to highlight the fact that there is *not* someone in a single person's life that has chosen to make the other person his/her top priority! And that even if there were someone in the past, they are no longer there.

Loneliness ran like an icy river through my soul, chilling me to the bone. My personal pain prevented me from looking around the room, but I envisioned other "Singles on Sunday" who were fighting a similar mental and emotional battle.

"If you are willing to make this commitment, as a couple, would you stand up right now?"

"Will you make a commitment to be more disciplined as a couple and commit to building more intimacy? Take each other's hands; look into each other's eyes…"

I continued, crumpled in my chair, tears streaming down my face… by the time the preacher reached the next invitation and explanation, my shell of self-protection was well in place, and I had almost completely tuned everything out.

He continued, "For those of you who are alone today, either your spouse isn't here, or you don't have one, please stand if you commit to greater discipline and having a conversation with a close friend or small group about it… if you can make the statement, 'I will commit to more discipline in the interest of cultivating more intimacy.'"

226 • ONE SINGLE REASON

From my fetal position, I wondered if I was simply too close to the trauma of my breakup to hear the words or if there were other women who were equally affected by this particular sermon. Later that day and through a small group Bible study that next Wednesday, I asked a few single girlfriends, in the most neutral way I knew how, "What did you think of Sunday's sermon? Did it affect you in any way?"

I wanted to let those ladies know that I cared how the sermon might've struck them, and I was also curious to know if my own reaction was disproportionate to the situation. Turns out it was a little bit of both. The majority of the women felt very uncomfortable, excluded, and hurt. It was a painful experience for most.

Personally, after attempting to return the following Sunday, I realized that I was going to be unable to continue to attend church during that sermon series. I chose, instead, to worship with the Hispanic congregation for the remaining Sundays of that series and was extremely grateful for the option to maintain the priority of worship and fellowship with other Christians, while still protecting myself from a more damaging than helpful topic.

My brokenness was too great at that time to process what I trust was a great series for the married couples.

Do I want marriages to be strengthened? Yes! Do I want the couples in our churches to be able to have a greater level of intimacy and trust in their marriages? Absolutely! However, on behalf of single and single-again women, I wondered if Sunday morning corporate worship service was the best setting for that series of lessons or not.

Once my emotions were more in check, I had a conversation with the preacher about that sermon series. He apologized profusely and affirmed that it was never his intention to isolate or hurt any single or single-again people in attendance. I told him that I accepted his apology and that I had already forgiven him.

He granted me permission to share this story even before I could reiterate that it would be relayed anonymously. He apologized again and said that he prayed that others would learn from his mistake, thanking me for bringing it to his attention.

Sisters, I encourage you to speak with your local preacher if you feel that single and/or single-again women are not properly represented or considered in the sermons. **Most of the preachers I have worked with and had the privilege of knowing do not have any intention of excluding others or hurting others through their lessons.** However, they may need to be made aware of the unique needs and perspectives of the single men and women in the congregation. I would rather you assume ignorance in a spirit of mutual edification than assume any sort of harmful intent. More often than not, we don't know what we don't know. We are all in this together and prayerfully walking with one another, supporting each other in the best ways we know how.

Supporting our Single Sisters

Out of concern for me as a single sister, the preacher's wife called me one Sunday afternoon. "Hey, Michelle. How are you? I'm just going to cut to the chase and let you know why I'm calling. Brother "Joe" was asking my husband and me about you the other day. He is recently divorced and has told us that he is looking to marry again. Preacher "Larry" is walking with Joe through this difficult time and I won't go into any details about the divorce, but I can say that he is definitely interested in you. We recognize that he can be awkward and does not pick up on social cues easily. I happened to see him talking to you across the way this morning. Did he say anything to you?"

"Oh yeah, he definitely did. He told me that he is recently single-again and that he is on the hunt. Yes, he used those words!"

"I'm so sorry."

"Yeah, I was shocked at first, but I was able to gather myself and let him know that I'm not interested. Thankfully, there was someone nearby I needed to talk to, so I excused myself and walked away. I was trying to be nice, but it was extremely awkward, especially because of how direct he was and the way he was looking at me."

"Again, I'm sorry. Neither Larry nor I want any of our single sisters to be uncomfortable coming to church here. As I mentioned, he does not understand subtlety or most social cues. You are going to have to be direct with him. I'm not asking you to be rude. I know you wouldn't be, but you do need to be direct if he talks to you again."

"Thank you for the suggestion and for that permission. Is that even the right word to use?"

"Sure. You definitely have our permission and our backing. If he does not understand that your "no means no," you just let me or Larry know and we will run interference. I'll keep my eye out. He's not dangerous or anything. We just want to make sure you are not put in a situation where you feel uncomfortable. Larry and Joe have the kind of a relationship where they can speak openly and directly. He is happy to talk with Brother Joe if anything else happens and you feel we need to step in."

"Thank you so much. I really appreciate your support. I did spend the rest of the time this morning trying to avoid wherever he was and avoid eye contact in order to not have to address things with him again."

"I understand. And you're welcome. Like I said, Preacher Larry and I want our single women to feel safe and to know that we are looking out for them."

I thanked the preacher's wife probably three more times before we hung up and asked her to pass on my thanks to the preacher. What might have been seen as a small gesture to some made a huge difference for me in feeling safe, supported, seen, and loved in my local congregation.

CHAPTER 28

Should We Start a Singles' Ministry?

²¹In him the whole building is joined together and rises to become a holy temple in the Lord. ²²And in him you too are being built together to become a dwelling in which God lives by his Spirit. (Eph. 2:21-22)

When approached by churches that are exploring the possibility of starting a Singles Ministry, the first question I ask them is, "How do you define singles?"

Remember, we could be talking about college students, those who went straight into the workforce after high school, young professionals, divorced, widowed, the socially single, the decidedly single, the "I wish with all my being I weren't single," and many others... Which group are you wanting to design your Singles Ministry for?

Each of the women whose stories have been shared highlight a different "single" dynamic—women with different needs, desires, challenges, and talents to offer.

The second question I ask is, "Have you talked with the singles in your congregation about this possibility? What do they say?"

229

For those who have a clear vision of what kind of singles ministry they want to start, as well as a team of singles who want to help make it happen, awesome! I pray God's blessings on your endeavor to facilitate a living out of our one single reason! May God bless the continued conversations and relationships with an overabundance of love and grace moving forward. As I tell anyone that travels with me internationally, "flexibility" needs to be your middle name.

There is no one perfect way to start, manage, or maintain a singles ministry if you do decide to promote one. Certain cities and certain church dynamics at a specific time in the life of a church can lend themselves to it being a successful program. But remember... Singles aren't a program, they are people. And people mean that it's all about relationship.

As a case study of one successful singles ministry, allow me to paint a picture...

Growing up, my dad was the deacon of the Singles Ministry. Bachelors would come over for Saturday morning waffles. Single women would babysit us girls. Visitors would join the large crowd for a backyard crawfish boil. Over time, some married, others remained single, and from both groups, we have been blessed to keep in touch with many.

Back in the 1980's and 1990's, a thriving and growing Campus Ministry facilitated a steady influx of graduates to the Singles Ministry, but it was not just a group of young professionals. There were truck drivers and skilled laborers. Single Christian men gave examples of what to or not to look for in a husband. Single Christian women told stories of the joys and the woes of being single. And I learned to appreciate and respect men and women who were more socially awkward.

In surveying some of the women who were a part of that group when I was a child, I asked "What was most impactful to you through that ministry?" or "What made it successful?" Every single one of their answers affirmed that "it's all about relationship."

Yes, singles were a normal and vital part of the church context where I grew up. However, as is the nature of any singles ministry, there are those that "graduate" either by getting married, moving away, or moving on, leaving others to stumble into navigating new relationships.

The turnover in a singles ministry is a natural byproduct of the ministry itself. And every time there is a significant turnover in a singles ministry, the ministry must redefine itself and build up new leaders. Turnover is a dynamic faced today among single adults in a congregation. We are more "mobile" and potentially have more flexibility to accept job transfers, pursue educational goals, or, of course, there will always be those who get married.

Most conversations that begin by asking about the formation of a Singles Ministry naturally transition to the next question:

Should We Have a Separate Bible Class for Singles?

In larger congregations, it is more feasible to offer a combination of classes for stages of life *and* topical classes, giving people the choice to join with those in a similar demographic or to discuss a book of the Bible, for example, with a more diverse group. In smaller congregations, there are fewer class options (strictly a numbers issue), which affords its own mix of pros and cons for how to provide options for Bible classes.

Without tallying exact quotes from the surveys, allow me to share four of the top quotes regarding the need for classes, activities, or programs specifically for singles of any type: "Have a singles class." "Don't have a separate singles class." "Give us time to be with people that understand." "Be sure and make all groups multi-generational and diverse."

Yep. The answers were all over the map. While the statements appear contradictory, they reflect the same sentiment: a deep desire for relationship, first with God, then with one another.

Relationship is the best fulfillment of our one single reason, showing love to every member of our local congregation through the study of God's Word together.

When asked about specific class options that would be helpful, a financial class was requested by multiple survey participants. This is a unique challenge for single income homes (whether single or single-again). The women also expressed a need for support in the areas of taking care of their cars, home repairs, etc.

And, as one sister expressed, "Single-again women need shame-free resources. Male preachers, pastors, and elders should frequently suggest PROFESSIONAL (not simply a mentor) connections to women going through anything difficult related to the female experience, but especially divorce."

As we have affirmed, most of the one-another passages in Scripture cannot be fulfilled sitting shoulder to shoulder on Sunday mornings, but rather are best exemplified between those corporate gatherings. Some single women feel lost in a sea of people in a larger congregational setting while others feel that the opportunity for connection and commonality was greater in a larger congregation. House churches and smaller congregations can provide more intimate bonds among a diverse group of people, but for those who are looking for a spouse, the smaller the group, the smaller the pool of possibilities.

Of course, Bible classes are not the only types of activities within the church. Are the Bible classes at your church (whether Sunday morning or any other time/setting) inclusive or exclusive of single and single-again women?

If women are expected to connect in Ladies' Bible Class, the only offering of those gatherings cannot be on Tuesday mornings when many women are working. Evening or weekend ladies' activities can be challenging for single moms who do not have a husband to take care of the children.

> Young single mom: "I can't participate in most women's events because there is nobody to watch my kids. The women I would ask are already participating in the event. It is assumed that a dad is available to help at home. Also, father/daughter and father/son events assume there is a father figure at home."

Until you get to know someone who has faced these challenges, there is no way you can learn to be sensitive to them. Thank you for picking up this book to engage in the conversation, develop these relationships, and live out your one single reason: love!

Remember: There is no perfect answer and no one who answered the surveys or were interviewed pretended to present a perfect solution. Yet we can engage in relationship and conversation with one another to facilitate a welcoming and supportive community in which we join together as one body.

For we are God's handiwork, created in Christ Jesus to do good works, which God prepared in advance for us to do. (Eph. 2:10)

CHAPTER 29

Church Family as Community

19 Consequently, you are no longer foreigners and strangers, but fellow citizens with God's people and also members of his household, 20 built on the foundation of the apostles and prophets, with Christ Jesus himself as the chief cornerstone. (Eph. 2:19-20)

The vast majority of the single women surveyed (79%) responded that they feel their local congregation includes them as a member of its family. However, only 61% feel that their local congregation is welcoming to single women. The following short answers and interviews provide insight into this 18% discrepancy. Of even greater value, these women share some specific suggestions.

When asked about how this single sister has best been supported—through family, individuals, groups, inside or outside the church—she answered:

It's primarily been specific individuals. **It's not that congregations haven't meant to be supportive, but it just hasn't been on their radar.** The period of my life where I felt most supported or most like a part of a specific group was actually whenever I was younger, whenever there were more women who were newly married or not married yet or in that life situation, so there was a group of us that had a weekly Bible

234

study. Whenever I was younger, those sorts of situations were much more common, and I felt much more a part of that community.

As I've gotten older, that group is not a match for my life situation, and there really isn't a group that matches the life situation that I am currently in... in any of the congregations that I've ever been a part of. So as a result of that, most of the support that I have felt has come from individuals—from those people who have included me as though I were biological family even though I'm not biological family.

Single mom: "Provide those casseroles for moms going through a divorce even if you aren't sure 'who's at fault.' And don't put us through a questionnaire. We've been through enough! We're drowning and trying to keep our kids from drowning!"

Angela R.: While everyone needs community, single adults often feel this need more acutely as they don't have the support of family nearby. This can be a great opportunity for the church to be the family of Christ in real and tangible ways. Invite singles to have lunch with you— leftovers on paper plates are fine—we just want to be a part of your family. Invite singles to sit with you during worship. It can be really intimidating to see all of the couples and families sitting in neat little rows. If you know a single is out with the flu, offer to pick up a prescription or bring them a meal. If a single misses church, send them a text to check on them. We might need help, and even if we don't, it's nice to know that someone notices whether or not we are there.

Angela B.: "Invite and include them in activities especially ones that are intergenerational and include families. [Singles] don't have a family at home, but they may want and need a family and can often feel excluded by so many things in the church that are family oriented whether it's intentionally family-oriented or not."

Kari H.: To be seen as on a long path of singleness, because you need to plan differently relationally, financially and in your education when singleness is the long view of your life. For example, more practical counsel on matters of living would have an added blessing in the church community. Thankfully, I have a great family. The church could have been a wonderful covenant community in those years, but I was mostly solicited for donations and volunteer time in those early years, rather than invested in one on one as a person on a valid lifelong journey of singleness with really specific challenges.

I appreciated one older single sister's insight and specificity, "Involve them in various committees, e.g., missions, search committee for minister, planning education curriculum." **Remember how much we all want a seat at the table and a voice in the conversation?** Thanks for including the single women's voices. Pray about the selection of every single person you want on those committees, just as I know you are praying over the other aspects of the conversations generated through this book.

When forming committees and gathering input from a cross-section of the congregation, please remember the significance of diversity. While this book's primary focus is on single and single-again women, we do not want their inclusion to be to the exclusion of any other under-represented group. We all want to be heard, valued, appreciated, and included.

One Final Statement

While it all comes back to love as our motivation, it also brings us back to the deepest desires of our heart: relationship and purpose.

There is no one cookie-cutter answer for all single and single-again women. While you're rolling out the dough and smoothing it to get nice, evenly cut cookies, the single woman is on the other side of the room making cake. The single mom is trying to keep her kids' fingers out of the batter. And the recently single-again sister is sitting in the corner, trying to remember if she ate breakfast.

Thanks for getting in the kitchen with us and being willing to get messy throughout this conversation. There are a few questions left for our Table Talk time. And the final Section is dedicated to Next Level Discussions which can help you facilitate these conversations in a small group context, as well as ask some of the same kinds of questions yourselves.

Table Talk

The Congregational Strategies are designed to be discussed conversationally. None of us should assume to have all the answers, nor should we fall into the trap of comparison between one congregation and another. We can learn from each other, but we must know and meet the needs in our local area.

I pray you will recommend this book as a tool for facilitating conversations and deepening relationships with members of your local congregation. There are many church leaders who want to learn how to better include single and single-again women in the congregation. Single ladies, God may be calling you to be a voice in that conversation.

If you would like additional resources for facilitating this discussion on a congregational level, please contact me at Iron Rose Sister Ministries. I would love to continue our conversation beyond the pages of this book, but I have thoroughly enjoyed engaging with you up to this point.

Talk with God (Reflection Questions)

What quote did you most "amen" and which one stepped the hardest on your toes?

Can you think of a time when you said something that was interpreted differently than how you meant it? What have you now learned about how you wish that conversation had gone differently?

How have you seen your church family live out love in community to a diverse group of individuals?

Talk with an Iron Rose Sister

 The **Common Threads** are a way to make any lesson personal and practical and are taken from the three parts of Iron Rose Sister Ministries' logo.

 An area in which you want to grow or bloom

 A thorn you'd like to remove (something hindering you from living out love in church contexts)

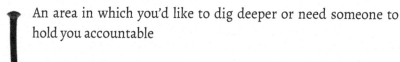 An area in which you'd like to dig deeper or need someone to hold you accountable

Table Talk with One Another (one-on-one or group discussion)

What has your local congregation done well in support of single women?

What is an area in which your local congregation can improve in welcoming or supporting single women?

What is your reaction to the contents of this section? Please explain where you are coming from in your reactions. As we dialogue about this, I want to hear you and I want you to hear me.

How have your insights or perceptions changed after discussing aspects of this section with someone else?

Walk the Talk

What is one single conversation to have with others, toward going deeper in understanding for your local congregation?

What is one single step you can take to help someone feel less "Solo on Sundays"?

Tips for Small Group Table Talk

Love, listen, and learn. Our conversation is about action steps and moving forward, not about airing past grievances. Remember, comparisons and assumptions are traps to avoid.

Inviting Church Leaders to the Table

One Single Reason: Congregational Strategies from Conversations with Single Women, is available as a stand-alone resource, specifically designed for church leaders. It contains the same content as Section VI, Congregational Strategies, in this book.

For additional information or to order the resource book for church leaders, you can visit https://ironrosesister.com/resources/store or use your phone to follow this QR code.

Section VII

Next Level Discussions

CHAPTER 30

Small Group Discussion Recommendations

There are multiple ways to use this book to facilitate a discussion of these topics in a small group setting.

- An intensive 6-week study, hitting the highlights of Sections I-VI.

- A 13-week discussion, selecting which chapters to combine for each week's discussion. This breaks down to 2-3 chapters per gathering.

Even if you do not feel equipped to facilitate the discussion or feel that you lack adequate experience to do so, it is a rich opportunity for growth and blessing. This book is all about facilitating the conversation.

You are among sisters and friends that are supporting you in this part of your journey, as well.

Suggestions for the Facilitator

➢ **Make it your own and allow the Spirit to lead—these studies are a resource, not a script.**
  - Select which Table Talk questions you would like to discuss, and plan for ones you might need to skip if you are

running short on time. You can also use questions that were presented within the chapters.

○ The Table Talk segment is designed to help facilitate the discussion.

▪ Table Talk with One Another and Walk the Talk are specifically designed to be used in a small group context.

▪ Don't insist that someone share their answers from the Talk with God (Reflection Questions), but they may allow for deeper discussion.

▪ It can be best to conclude with the Common Threads (Talk with an Iron Rose Sister) since the conversation as a group may enlighten or inform additional areas in which someone wants to grow.

▪ Section-specific suggestions are included as part of the Tips for Small Group Table Talk portion.

○ You are welcome to add questions of your own or highlight portions of the chapters that most impacted you.

○ Note: More times than not, for time reasons, you will not be able to cover *every* question in the entire section together each week. Pray and prioritize. Be willing to continue the conversation outside of the formal gathering.

➢ **Include additional examples from Scripture and encourage others to do the same.**

○ Avoid a tendency to "preach" on this topic. We are facilitating a conversation.

○ Online Bible programs such as BibleGateway.com or BlueLetterBible.org provide excellent resources like multiple versions of the Bible, concordances (to look up the occurrences of a word), Bible dictionaries, and commentaries.

➢ **Be willing to answer the designated discussion questions first, using your own examples, but avoid the temptation to do all the talking.**

o Allow for awkward silence to provide the opportunity for others to share. Tip: Counting to 10 in your head gives others a chance to think about their answers. Feel free to reword the question, as well.

o It's okay to call on someone and encourage them to answer a specific question.

o "Can you expound on that?" or "Can you add to that comment?" are good follow-up questions for discussion.

➢ **Leading is about facilitating the conversation, not about having all the answers.**

o When someone brings up a difficult situation or a challenging question, you can always open it up to the group for answers from Scripture, not personal advice.

o The answer may merit further Bible study or the consultation of someone with more experience in the Word and/or experience regarding that type of situation. That's okay! We're digging deeper in our Table Talk and having next level discussions.

➢ **Affirm and encourage group participation.**

o One of the best ways to facilitate respectful, genuine discussion is to affirm the others in the group any time they contribute to the conversation. Even if you don't agree with what is stated, you can appreciate their willingness to share their thoughts.

o Thank those who were willing to read passages of Scripture, to pray, and to ask questions. Each are contributions to the conversation. And don't forget to thank those who participated by sharing their answers and input during the discussion.

○ If someone is talking too much or over-sharing, you can gently interrupt and thank her for sharing. It may be appropriate to lead a prayer over the individual or the situation in that moment to move forward with the topic.

➢ **Accommodate for larger groups, as needed.**

○ The ideal small group size is 6-8 individuals. If your group is larger, more reserved people will be less likely to share.

○ For groups larger than 6-8, in order to facilitate a deeper connection with one another and with God, here are a few suggestions:

▪ Choose a section of the chapter or specific questions that can be answered in mini-groups (2-3 people).

▪ Allow for time in those mini-group discussions and then bring the entire group back together. This can be done multiple times during the conversation.

▪ Also, the mini-groups can be a good way to share in the Common Threads and/or in prayer.

➢ **Give a practical wrap-up conclusion or way to Walk the Talk (an action step application from the discussion).**

➢ **Be sure to budget some time for prayer.**

➢ **Remember our purposes as students of the Word and daughters of the King.** We are striving to love, listen, learn, and to deepen our relationships with God and one another, especially single and single-again women. We want to foster an environment that inspires us to be Iron Rose Sisters, serving as iron sharpening iron as we encourage one another to be as beautiful as a rose in spite of a few thorns.

Initial Survey Questions

The snowball method was used to find female, single or single-again participants. Two hundred and twenty (220) total women participated: 165 in English and 55 in Spanish. Frequencies of their answers to Questions 3-12 are included below, listed below the question, as asked via Survey Monkey.

Logistical Questions from the Initial Survey have been removed for the summary in this book context. Complete surveys are available at https://IronRoseSister.com/single/.

*3. Year you were born: _____

    10%, 1936-1955   16%, 1956-1970   12%, 1971-1980   15%, 1981-1985

    14%, 1986-1990   15%, 1991-1995   17%, 1996-2001

*4. Current Status (choose one):

    71%, Single (never married)

    29%, Single-again, total from below

    [12%, Separated   64%, Divorced 22%, Widowed 2%, Other]

*5. Are you a parent or guardian?   28%, Yes   72%, No

*6. Where did you grow up?   73% in the U.S.

    27% in a country other than the U.S. (primarily Latin America)

*7. Where you reside (U.S. state or country outside the U.S.):

    This data point was not statistically significant for any answers.

*8. Primary language spoken in your childhood home:

    71%, English   27%, Spanish   1%, Other (please specify):

*9. What best describes the church in which you grew up?

66%, Non-denominational: Church of Christ

7%, Non-denominational: Not assoc. with Churches of Christ

7%, Catholic

15%, Protestant/Evangelical

2%, Other

3%, None

*10. What best describes the church where you currently attend?

70%, Non-denominational: Church of Christ

10%, Non-denominational: Not assoc. with Churches of Christ

1%, Catholic

10%, Protestant/Evangelical

6%, Other

3%, None

*11. Size of the congregation where you currently attend:

15%, 1-50   15%, 51-100   16%, 101-200   28%, 201-500   25%, 500+

*12. Would you like to get married?

10%, No, thanks   41%, Maybe   49%, Yes, please!

> ***NOTE: For space reasons, frequency answers***
> ***to Questions 13-18 are available on our website.***

*13. On a scale of 'Strongly Disagree' to 'Strongly Agree', indicate how much you agree with the following statements (Circle one):

[options provided for each question]

Strongly Disagree	*Disagree*	*Agree*	*Strongly Agree*	*Non-applicable*

- I am content in my singleness.
- My relationship with God has been strengthened through my time as a single woman.
- As a single woman, my relationships with other Christian women have been strengthened.

*14. Rank the following groups from Most Supportive to Least Supportive of you as a single Christian woman (1 = Most Supportive, 6 = Least Supportive):

_____ Family

_____ Friends

_____ Local community (e.g. sports, book club, supper club, service organization, etc.)

_____ Local congregation

_____ Online community (e.g. Facebook, gaming, dating sites, etc.)

_____ Work or academic community

*15. On a scale from 'Highly Encouraging' to 'Highly Discouraging,' rate the following groups according to how positively or negatively their remarks affect you as a single Christian woman (Circle one):

[options provided for each question]

| Highly encouraging | Encouraging | Discouraging | Highly discouraging | N/A |

[same groups as in Question 14]

*16. On a scale of 'Strongly Disagree' to 'Strongly Agree', indicate how much you agree with the following statements:

[4 selection options provided for each question, as listed in Question 13]

- As a single Christian woman, it is easy to find ways to serve within my local congregation.
- It is easier for a single Christian man to find a way to serve within my local congregation than for a single Christian woman.
- It is easier for a single Christian man to find his place in a work or academic environment than for a single Christian woman.
- It is easier for a married Christian woman to find a way to serve within my local congregation than for a single Christian woman.
- It is easier for a married Christian woman to find her place in a work or academic environment than for a single Christian woman.

*17. Which one(s) of the following statements are true?
(Check all that apply.)

____ My local congregation includes me as a member of its family.

____ My local congregation accepts my status as a single woman.

____ My local congregation is welcoming to single women.

____ I have observed other congregations providing support for single women.

____ None of these statements are true.

*18. On a scale of "Always" to "Never" (4 selection options), please
indicate how often you have experienced the following (Circle one):
[options provided for each question]

| | Always | Frequently | Occasionally | Never |

- How often have you been <u>negatively</u> affected by comments made by those in <u>society</u> about your singleness?
- How often have you been <u>negatively</u> affected by comments made by those in your <u>family</u> about your singleness?
- How often have you been <u>negatively</u> affected by comments made by those in the <u>church</u> about your singleness?
- How often have you been <u>positively</u> affected by comments made by those in <u>society</u> about your singleness?
- How often have you been <u>positively</u> affected by comments made by those in your <u>family</u> about your singleness?
- How often have you been <u>positively</u> affected by comments made by those in the <u>church</u> about your singleness?

Tell Us More!

> *NOTE: The following short answer Questions from*
> *the Initial Survey were optional. Anonymous answers to*
> *Questions 19-24 are available on our website.*

19. What is the most negative remark you have heard about "being single"?

20. What is the most positive remark you have heard about "being single"?

21. What is the greatest challenge as a single Christian woman?

22. What is the greatest blessing as a single Christian woman?

23. Please share a specific recommendation for one way in which the church can show its support for single or single-again women.

24. Is there anything else you would like to share here?

CHAPTER 32

Follow-up Survey Questions

Twenty-seven (27) women answered a minimum of two Follow-up Survey questions in English. The eight (8) Spanish participants of the Follow-up Survey were evaluated separately. Answers to both sets of Follow-Up Surveys are available on our website.

Initial and Final Logistical Questions have been removed for this summary. The full survey is available at https://IronRoseSister.com/single/.

1.   Please share a specific Bible verse that has encouraged you as a single woman. *(Shared in Section II, Chapter 8.)*

2.   What has your experience been with "Singles Ministry"?

3.   Tell us a little about your story as a single woman.

4.   If not mentioned specifically in the previous question, how have you served the Lord through your time as a single woman?

Or how would you like to (through your gifts, talents, and experiences)?

5. FOR SINGLE WOMEN, NEVER MARRIED: Besides the need to get married, your status as a single woman, or other related remarks, what things would you like for people to discuss with you?

6. FOR SINGLE-AGAIN WOMEN: What help or support did you most need from others when you first became single-again?

7. Any tips for other single women about how you have learned to respond to remarks about "being single"?

CHAPTER 33

Interview Questions

Interviews were conducted in public venues (e.g., coffee shops), were audio recorded with the participant's permission, and were conducted in a casual, conversational manner. Questions were not necessarily asked in the order listed. At times, a question was skipped if the respondent had already spoken to that topic with a previous answer. Interviewees were given the option to share their name or to participate anonymously.

Five formal interviews were conducted in English, plus four formal interviews in Spanish.

1. Can you tell me a little about yourself? What three words best describe you? What's really important to being you?

2. Tell me a little about your story as a single woman.

3. Can you walk me through a specific story or experience that has made a significant impact on you as a single woman? (It's okay to share more than one.)

4. What effects have you experienced your singleness having on your relationship with God?

5. What has been your experience in relationships with other Christian women?

6. What has God said or taught you, or what direction has He led you, through your time as a single woman?

7. How have you been best supported in your singleness—by individuals, by groups, inside or outside the church?

8. How can the church best be welcoming to single women?

9. Anything else you would like to add or wish that I had asked?

CHAPTER 34

About Iron Rose Sister Ministries

I f you would like to schedule a conference on this topic with Michelle J. Goff, please contact info@ironrosesister.com.

This speaker package can also include separate meetings or question and answer periods with single adults and church leaders in the congregation.

Our Purpose

Iron Rose Sister Ministries (IRSM) exists to equip women to connect to God and one another more deeply across the Americas.

We **equip** women through Bible study materials, seminars, mentoring relationships, and other resources to connect to God and one another more deeply. We **encourage** women to look to God and His Word through the one-another relationships God designed for His church. And we **empower** women to take ownership of their own spiritual walk.

Why

In a world where we are highly "connected," there is a lack of depth to our relationships with God and with one another as women. A lack of equipping resources prompted Michelle J. Goff to answer the call with, "Here am I, send me!" (Is. 6:8), launching Iron Rose Sister Ministries in order to

- facilitate Christian sister relationships that are like iron sharpening iron (Prov. 27:17), encouraging each other to be as beautiful as a rose, in spite of a few thorns.

- develop, write, and publish women's Bible studies simple enough for anyone to lead and deep enough for everyone to grow.

- create a network of Christian women and women's ministries across the Americas.

- conduct events across the Americas, teaching, empowering, and inspiring women on their journey as Iron Rose Sisters.

Where

Since its beginning in July 2013, God has opened doors for IRSM to encourage, equip, and empower women in more than half of the states in the U.S., all 19 Spanish-speaking countries of Latin America, and Portuguese-speaking Brazil, as well as Angola and Mozambique (in Africa).

We partner with the local congregation in the target areas, submitting to the local leadership, while equipping the women in their relationships with God and one another.

Spanish: Ministerio Hermana Rosa de Hierro

Portuguese: Ministêrio Irmã Rosa de Ferro

Who

The **Ministry Team** is made up of part-time and full-time workers across the U.S. (bios on website). **Volunteers and Ministry Reps** actively participate from each of the countries we serve.

Our **Board of Directors** always includes at least one elder, a mix of ages and areas of expertise, and a combination of men and women, all passionate about equipping women. We also function under the oversight of an **advisory eldership**.

We have a growing group of **Speakers, Authors, and Mentors** across the Americas fulfilling the vision God has given us.

Michelle J. Goff, *Founder, Author, International Speaker*

Michelle has always been passionate about equipping English- and Spanish-speaking women in their walks with God through speaking, writing, teaching, and mentoring. Her years of experience in women's and campus ministries, church-planting, domestic and foreign missions have prepared her to share these resources on a global level with women through IRSM.

Iron Rose Sister Ministries is a registered 501(c)(3) corporation. To learn more, pray with us, or give toward the vision God has given us, please visit our website: https://IronRoseSister.com/.

Acknowledgements

First and foremost, thanks to God who has walked with me every step of the way to make this project a reality and has patiently transformed me in the process. He has lived out love in my life, in many ways and through many people. The following list is only a small sample of the countless people who have exemplified their one single reason.

To the 220 women who participated in the Initial Survey, both in English and Spanish, your words may not be quoted, but your voices were heard. Thank you!

And to the Follow-up Survey participants, those interviewed (officially and unofficially), and to the women over the years whose voices have each formed a part of the conversation shared through this book, you were heard, and your input is valued.

To the women of the pilot study who stayed with me through the end, even when we had to switch to Zoom because of a global pandemic. Thank you!

Tremendous thanks and heartfelt love to the following people specifically:

David and Jocelynn Goff for dropping everything to join me on the final day of my initial writing retreat so that I could "talk it out." You have always made sure that I never feel alone.

David and Vanessa Gilliam for granting me access to their lake house as a quiet retreat for writing.

The Iron Rose Sister Ministries Team: Brenda Brizendine, Melanie Curtis, Katie Forbess, Wendy Neill, Amanda Nitsch, and Anna Sumner for holding down the fort in my absence and for allowing me to set the boundary of focusing on writing one day per week.

The Iron Rose Sister Ministries Board for supporting the vision of this book and for always striving to equip more women to connect to God and one another more deeply.

Jordan Yarbrough for serving as a captive audience as I read sections aloud.

Naomi Sechrest for serving as a sounding board and reviewer.

My research partners and transcribers: Rachel Baker and Liliana Henríquez. Thanks for sticking with me!

Dr. Anessa Westbrook and Dr. Susan Shirel for being champions of me and of this cause, for their research-savvy advice, and for their voices in this conversation.

Dr. James Huff for his counsel on the interviews and qualitative analyses.

Dr. Débora Rodrigo for guiding me through the statistical analysis and to the JASP creators for their software.

Abigail Baumgartner for her SAS statistical analyses, her input, and her diligence as my first "writing intern."

Beta readers, final proofers, reviewers, and many other volunteers who made the paperback book possible: Abby, Amanda, Amy, Angela, Carla, Chelsea, Chrys, David, Jessica, Jocelynn, Kara, Liliana, Katie, Naomi, Rachel, Robin, and Vicky. Thank you!

Ken Mills for his patience in developing the cover design.

And finally, to Renata Arandia López, for the bio photo.

Author's Final Note

Through *One Single Reason* and the subsequent conversations with single and single again women, **it is my prayer that *"your love may abound more and more, in knowledge and depth of insight"* (Phil. 1:9), as we live out that love, our one single reason**. Every single one of us has a longing to know and be known, to love and be loved through relationship and purpose—the deepest desires of our hearts.

To that end, may we continue to support one another through Prayer, Encouragement, Activities, and Reminders of Truth. May God guide us to avoid the traps of Comparisons, Assumptions, Judgements, and Expectations. May we respond in ways that leads to contentment through Acknowledging the Disappointment, Protecting Ourselves, Thanking God, Loving Others, and Yearning for the Right Things.

I know I am not the only one who is Single and Lovin' It, Mostly, nor am I the only one who longs to facilitate more conversations about strategies we can employ in a congregational context to help single and single-again women feel seen, welcomed, encouraged, and supported.

Thank you for being willing to join the conversation by pulling up a chair to the table. Now it's time to walk the talk and invite others to the Lord's Table by living out His love.

Michelle J. Goff